Content

ISBN: 978 1 80282 758 3
Editor: Jon Lake
Senior editor, specials: Roger Mortimer
Email: roger.mortimer@keypublishing.com
Cover design: Steve Donovan
Design: SJmagic DESIGN SERVICES, India
Advertising Sales Manager: Brodie Baxter
Email: brodie.baxter@keypublishing.com
Tel: 01780 755131
Advertising Production: Debi McGowan
Email: debi.mcgowan@keypublishing.com

SUBSCRIPTION/MAIL ORDER
Key Publishing Ltd, PO Box 300,
Stamford, Lincs, PE9 1NA
Tel: 01780 480404
Subscriptions email: subs@keypublishing.com
Mail Order email: orders@keypublishing.com
Website: www.keypublishing.com/shop

PUBLISHING
Group CEO: Adrian Cox
Publisher, Books and Bookazines:
Jonathan Jackson
Published by
Key Publishing Ltd, PO Box 100,
Stamford, Lincs, PE9 1XQ
Tel: 01780 755131 **Website:** www.
keypublishing.com

PRINTING
Precision Colour Printing Ltd, Haldane,
Halesfield 1, Telford, Shropshire. TF7 4QQ

DISTRIBUTION
Seymour Distribution Ltd, 2 Poultry
Avenue, London, EC1A 9PU
Enquiries Line: 02074 294000.

At one time, the USAF expected to field an all-stealthy frontline fast jet force. Here F-22 Raptors from the 94th Fighter Squadron at Joint Base Langley-Eustis, and F-35 Lightning IIs from the 58th Fighter Squadron, at Eglin Air Force Base, fly in formation over the Eglin Training Range after completing an integration training mission on November 5, 2014. (Photo: US Air Force, Master Sgt Shane A. Cuomo)

From seven types to four

Today the USAF's fighter force consists of a disparate mix of aircraft types – some of which are now quite old. There are urgent plans to recapitalise the fighter fleet with a mix of new and upgraded types, as part of a wider effort to reconfigure America's forces to meet a new and rapidly changing geo-strategic environment.

The end of the Cold War saw the US reduce its armed forces in size, in response to what was expected to be the disappearance of the old Soviet threat. Expectations of a 'peace dividend' saw military budgets cut back, and efforts to re-equip and recapitalise different force elements were slowed down or cancelled.

The 1991 Gulf War seemed to show that small numbers of new, high tech weapons and platforms would, in future, achieve mission success that would have previously required significant mass. It was calculated in the USAF's report 'Reaching Globally, Reaching Powerfully: The United States Air Force in the Gulf War' that: "In World War II it could take 9,000 bombs to hit a target the size of an aircraft shelter. In Vietnam, 300. Today we can do it with one laser-guided munition from an F-117."

The 1990s saw the USAF engaged in a succession of campaigns against sub-peer opponents – primarily in Iraq and the Balkans, none of which provided much impetus for significant improvements to the fighter force. With the attacks against the World Trade Center and Pentagon on September 11, 2001, the US launched the so-called War on Terror.

This consisted of a series of asymmetric counter insurgency campaigns which saw the USAF's fighter force reduced to flying relatively unchallenging Close Air Support missions, with little opportunity to exercise higher-end warfighting skills.

But while the post 9/11 fighter fleet was not undertaking particularly demanding mission sets, the operational tempo was high, and the fleet of legacy 4th generation fighter aircraft soon started to show adverse effects from the frequent deployments and heavy use. In May 2009, the Congressional Budget Office (CBO) reported that F-35 production rates over the

Almost incredibly, the world's most capable fighter, Lockheed Martin's superlative F-22, will be among the first fighter types to disappear from the USAF's inventory. Whatever emerges from the NGAD programme has big shoes to fill! (Photo: US Air Force)

The similarities and differences between the F-22 (nearest) and the F-35A are shown to advantage in this view of a Langley-based Raptor and an F-35A from Hill AFB. (Photo: US Air Force)

next 25 years would be insufficient to keep pace with the rate at which 4th generation fighter aircraft were wearing out.

This had been dramatically demonstrated on November 2, 2007, when a 27-year-old F-15C assigned to the 131st Fighter Wing (80-0034) broke up during air combat manoeuvring training near St. Louis, Missouri. The aircraft

'broke in half' after the failure of one of four forward fuselage longerons due to fatigue cracking. Fortunately, the pilot, Major Stephen W. Stilwell, was able to eject, though he suffered injuries.

The F-15C/D fleet was grounded, pending inspection, and though most returned to flight, some were deemed to be beyond economic

repair, and others had new flight restrictions imposed. During his testimony to Congress in May 2009, General Norton A. Schwartz, the then USAF chief of staff, stated that: "Our ageing air and space fleet requires focused attention," noting that all legacy fighter types (F-16, F-15, and A-10) had been grounded during the previous two years.

>

An F-35 Lightning II, F-22 Raptor and two F-5 Tigers fly in formation during the Heritage Flight Training Course at Davis-Monthan Air Force Base, Arizona, on March 4, 2023. The F-5E remains a potent adversary aircraft, while the related T-38 frequently serves as a companion trainer. (Photo: US Air Force, Airman 1st Class Paige Weldon)

Despite the overstretch and high operational tempo, some pressed for a reduction in the fighter fleet, calculating that early retirement of 250 legacy fighters could save $3.5bn over the next five years, redistributing that funding to higher priority missions while building a smaller, more capable force. The justification was that this kind of restructuring plan would "eliminate excessive overmatch in our tactical fighter force," and that the "force structure announcement reflects our best effort to meet the expanding Air Force mission areas and growing joint demands."

Before the FY2010 defence budget, the CBO published its *Alternatives for Modernizing US Fighter Forces* study, which considered a number of options, including the purchase of advanced versions of legacy fighters, including an F-16 upgraded with "improved avionics, AESA radar, conformal fuel tanks for longer flight range, and a strengthened airframe for carrying larger payloads."

In the FY2010 defence budget itself, Congress mandated a follow-on study looking at the number of 4.5 generation fighter aircraft that would need to be procured between fiscal years 2011 and 2025 in order to meet the requirement to maintain not less than 2,200 tactical fighter aircraft.

But the importance of tactical aircraft continued to reduce as larger platforms became more highly prized, thanks to their longer range and endurance, and thanks to the greater persistence arising from their bigger payloads. This did not, however, result in any reduction in workload on the USAF fighter force, which became increasingly over-stretched and stressed. At the same time, there was a growing interest in dedicated light attack aircraft (though

a number of US light attack programmes failed to reach fruition), and in unmanned systems, whose very long endurance made them especially useful for gathering 'pattern of life' ISR and for attacking fleeting insurgent targets.

On June 26, 2009, the USAF released a force structure plan that cut fighter aircraft and shifted resources to better support for nuclear, irregular and information warfare, but there was a growing resistance to force reductions and a growing demand for fighter force improvements. The 2008 National Defense Strategy identified Russia, China, Iran, and North Korea (the remaining 'Axis of Evil' nations) as the primary threats to US security

interests. Some far-sighted observers detected in the 2008 war with Georgia, a resurgence of an expansionist/nationalist Russian threat. There was also a renewal of Russian bomber penetrations into the Alaskan Air Defense Zone. The Russian invasion of Crimea in 2014 further underlined the changing threat.

Rationalisation

The USAF is planning to rationalise its fighter fleet from seven aircraft types to just four and will jettison the A-10 and the F-22 in the process. This plan forms part of a wider initiative that is aimed at rebalancing the USAF's frontline in order to keep pace and compete with China. Today's fighter fleet includes the F-22A, the F-35A, the F-16C/D, the F-15C/D, the F-15E, and the A-10A, and will transition to a fleet consisting of F-35As, F-16s, F-15E/EX Eagles and the new NGAD fighter.

Last December, the US Government Accountability Office (GAO) published a report into Tactical Aircraft Investments, noting that:

"Most of DoD's existing tactical aircraft first entered service in the 1970s and 1980s and have exceeded their original service lives. As DoD seeks to modernize its tactical aircraft fleet, it must balance sustaining older aircraft currently in operation with developing and procuring more advanced capabilities to support the future force."

The report acknowledged that: "Recent studies conducted by the Department of Defense's Joint Staff and the military services have found that DoD needs to modernize its tactical aircraft fleet. Seven of eight studies found that existing aircraft did not have the capabilities needed to compete in future combat scenarios and some noted the need to invest in advanced technologies to address future needs."

But the report also highlighted a lack of transparency in the USAF's plans, which, it averred, was likely to lead to poorly informed decision-making, with potential for wasting money and duplicating effort.

"The lack of an integrated acquisition portfolio review of tactical aircraft platforms leaves DoD and Congress with limited insight into interdependencies, risks and related trade-offs among some of DoD's highest priority and most expensive investments," the report stated.

"Without an analysis of the tactical aircraft platform portfolio and a requirement to report underlying information externally, DoD and Congress will continue to have limited information when making major investment decisions."

Built for a different time

General Mark Kelly, the commander of Air Combat Command, used his keynote address to the Air Force Association Air, Space and

Despite its size and power, the USAF relies on support from regional allies. Here a Republic of Singapore Air Force A330 Multi Role Tanker Transport leads a formation flight with a US Air Force F-16C Fighting Falcon assigned to the 36th Fighter Squadron, Osan Air Base, South Korea, a South Korean F-15K and a Royal Thai Air Force F-16B during exercise Cope Tiger 23 over Korat Royal Thai Air Base, Kingdom of Thailand, March 22, 2023. (Courtesy Photo)

Not all of the USAF's partners operate the same aircraft types. Here a US Air Force F-35A Lightning II, two Dassault Rafales and a Royal Air Force Eurofighter Typhoon break formation over France on May 19, 2021. The flight was a part of the Atlantic Trident 21 exercise which was a joint, multinational exercise involving service members from the US, France, and the UK, and was aimed at enhancing fourth- and fifth-generation integration, combat readiness and fighting capabilities, through conducting complex air operations in a contested multinational joint force environment. (Photo: US Air Force, Staff Sgt Alexander Cook)

Cyber Conference, on September 22, 2022, to acknowledge that today's fighter force had been designed for a different peer adversary, and had been built for a different time. He acknowledged that they had been used in a different way than had originally been planned and said that the proposed changes were urgently required.

The seven-fleet fighter force was itself something of an accident of history. At the height of the Cold War, the USAF had planned for an 'all-Stealth' force, with a fighter fleet consisting of F-22s and F-35s, and with an all B-2 bomber force. Budgetary constraints and a changing strategic environment saw this ambitious plan being abandoned, and the teen-series fighters and the A-10 enjoyed longer careers than were once envisaged. These fighters proved themselves better suited to the asymmetric and counterinsurgency air campaigns that characterised the post-Cold War era than

the newer fifth generation fighters, and their shortcomings were less apparent as the USAF shifted its focus away from major near-peer adversaries.

But in 2018, the US DoD's primary strategy document, the National Defense Strategy, signalled a shift away from a focus on counterinsurgency and combatting violent extremism. Instead, the US DoD realigned its sights on the challenges of peer-level warfare, and on the growing threat posed ➤

Forty-nine F-16 Vipers and MQ-9 Reapers assigned to the 49th Wing line up on the runway during an elephant walk at Holloman Air Force Base, New Mexico, April 21, 2023. The 49th Wing is the US Air Force's largest F-16 and MQ-9 formal training unit, building combat aircrew pilots and sensor operators ready for any future conflicts. Unmanned platforms look set to play an increasingly important role in the future. (Photo: US Air Force, Tech Sgt Victor J. Caputo)

Major Joshua 'Cabo' Gunderson, F-22 Raptor Demonstration Team commander, performs at the Thunder Over New Hampshire Air Show at Pease Air National Guard Base on September 11, 2021. The unmatched manoeuvrability of the air force's fifth-generation air dominance stealth fighter is matched by very high speed, stealth, and sensor performance. (US Air National Guard photo by Tech Sgt Steven Tucker)

by major powers, recognising the challenge to US prosperity and security posed by long-term, strategic competition with Putin's Russia and Xi Xin Ping's China, who have actively sought to undermine US military advantages.

In an age of rapid technological change, accompanied by increasing uncertainty and complexity, the US military advantage is being eroded, and the nation can no longer take for granted the unchallenged military dominance it has enjoyed for the last three decades.

Now that the USAF is facing the growing possibility of having to fight a peer level opponent, the balance is shifting back in favour of the low observable (stealthy) F-35, though there has been a recognition that non-stealthy platforms may still have a useful part to play. But US Air Force Chief of Staff General Charles Q Brown, Jnr has said that the air force must prioritise the cutting-edge capabilities that will be able to survive in contested airspace and that will keep the service ahead of the "pacing threat", which is now seen as being China.

"We have to focus our fighter force to face the realities of a new threat environment," Mark Kelly has noted. "Our fighter force was designed for a Soviet force. We are behind and our current

incremental rate of change is insufficient. Fighter Roadmap is a change in investment priorities required for a peer fight. The fighter force will again need to flex from its original design to defeat a peer threat. We need to face the realities of a new threat environment and that requires the fighter force to change."

"We have to be able to compete and fight well beyond the permissive counterinsurgency environments we've operated in for the last 20 years," Kelly believes. "If you're going to be an air force that flies, fights and wins anytime, anywhere, the anywhere includes the highly contested sovereigns," Kelly said, noting that: "It is significantly harder to compete against a nation in their own sovereign space." To win against a near-peer adversary like China or Russia, Kelly says that the US needs "high

US Air Force Maj Kristin Wolfe performs a demonstration in the F-35A Lightning II during at the Reno Air Races in Reno, Nevada, September 19, 2021. The F-35 Lightning II has many of the same attributes as the F-22 but cannot supercruise. *(Photo: US Air Force, Tech Sgt Nicolas Myers)*

Eighteen US Air Force F-35A Lightning IIs and 12 F-16 Fighting Falcons assigned to the 354th Fighter Wing and two KC-135 Stratotankers assigned to the 168th Wing perform an elephant walk at Eielson Air Force Base, Alaska, December 18, 2020. The F-16 and F-35 form the backbone of the USAF's tactical aircraft fleet. *(Photo: US Air Force, Senior Airman Beaux Hebert)*

capability, high capacity and affordability," which "takes a range of capabilities."

Some believe that the distances involved in the Pacific theatre, coupled with China's formidable A2AD (Anti-Access/Area Denial) capabilities may make the use of tactical aircraft difficult, and that longer range platforms with very long range stand-off weapons may dominate any air campaign against China.

Whether or not this is the case, winning against China and Russia will require US forces to strike diverse targets (including mobile targets) in highly contested environments, protected by the enemy's air defence and surface to air missile defence networks. This will require urgent change at a significant scale and the 2018 National Defense Strategy warned that failure to achieve this would rapidly result in a force that would be irrelevant to the threat.

General Brown's strategy document, *Accelerate Change or Lose* noted that "Good enough today will fail tomorrow." Kelly noted that: "When it comes to modern combat, if you don't like change, you're going to really dislike irrelevance, and you're going to outright hate a kinetic defeat."

To avoid this, the air force will need tactical aircraft with more advanced capabilities, as well as improved air-to-air refuelling capabilities, enhanced connectivity, and battlespace awareness, but mass is also vitally important.

"The Fighter Roadmap is part of the change you must make or lose. We must have the right-sized fleet to keep viable," Kelly said. The US Air Force operated a fleet of about 4,000 tactical fast jets and 134 fighter squadrons when it undertook Operation Desert Storm in 1991, but 30 years on, that inventory has reduced to around 2,000 aircraft, with 48 fighter squadrons (and nine attack squadrons). The

air force is statutorily required to maintain a minimum of 1,145 fighter aircraft in its primary mission aircraft inventory, and US Air Force officials have said that a minimum of 2,100 tactical aircraft would be sufficient to meet future needs, though there is an acknowledgement that the air force found that fifth- and sixth-generation aircraft should allow the service to meet its mission with fewer aircraft than are in the current inventory. The US Navy and Marine Corps want another 1,200 fighters. Some believe that the US fighter fleet is already too small, and though the air force's own study of its tactical air requirements is classified, Kelly has endorsed the conclusions of the 2018 *Air Force We Need* study, which called for a 62 squadron fighter force.

Sustainment costs

Overall numbers aside, there is a compelling case for reducing the number of aircraft types in service, to reduce support and sustainment costs, while withdrawing the oldest airframes in order to reduce the average age of the fleet. Many of the USAF's fixed-wing fighter aircraft are becoming increasingly more expensive and difficult to maintain as they face issues with diminishing manufacturing sources and systems/parts obsolescence. Mission capable rates have also proved disappointing – especially for the F-35, which forms the cornerstone of the USAF tactical aircraft fleet, but also for the USAF's older aircraft types.

To address future capability gaps while maintaining acquisition and sustainment affordability, the USAF aims to divest some fourth generation tactical aircraft - specifically, the A-10 and F-15C/D, and to redirect funding for these types to fund development of the NGAD system of systems.

To recapitalise the fighter fleet while reducing the number of types in service, without further eroding overall numbers is a tough challenge, and one that will require heavy investment, and a steady flow of new aircraft. The air force has calculated that it will need to buy at least 72 new fighters each year if it is to reach the force levels required, with the right capabilities. For many years Congress has approved fighter procurements that are lower than the air force's requested totals and has also stood in the way of divestment plans – especially in the case of the A-10. There are some signs that this may be changing. The FY23 budget request originally asked for 57 fighters – consisting of 33 F-35As and 24 F-15EXs with seven additional F-35As in an unfunded priorities list. Congress eventually approved a total of 43 F-35As (three more than requested), along with 24 F-15EX Eagle IIs, giving a total of 67 fighters.

The USAF's FY 2024 budget proposal (released in March) asked for 48 new F-35As and 24 F-15EXs – 72 fighters, and Lieutenant General Richard Moore, the air force's deputy chief of staff for plans and programs, said that this level of request is not a "one-time thing."

But while this level of procurement is sustainable while the US has what Moore called "two hot fighter production lines," once F-15EX procurement is complete (and under current plans the final 24 will be requested in FY 2025), it will rely on Lockheed Martin's ability to build 72 F-35As for the US Air Force each year, in addition to aircraft for a growing list of export customers, unless NGAD production is beginning by then, which seems unlikely.

Gen Moore said that the US defence-industrial base has limitations, and that the COVID-19 pandemic caused lingering

An F-22A Raptor from Langley Air Force Base, a QF-4E Phantom from Holloman Air Force Base, an F-16C Fighting Falcon, and an A-10A Thunderbolt II fly in diamond formation over Tucson, Arizona, on March 5, 2006. Remarkably, the A-10 and F-22 will soon follow the F-4 into retirement, but the F-16's future is assured. (Photo: US Air Force, Tech Sgt Ben Bloker)

A formation of fourth-generation fighter jets from the 40th Flight Test Squadron flies near Eglin Air Force Base, Florida on January 31, 2022. An A-10C leads an F-16C and F-15EX, which are flanked by an F-15C and an F-15E. The USAF's Roadmap will see the retirement of the F-15C, and the A-10C. (Photo: US Air Force, Tech Sgt John Raven)

supply chain and workforce issues that could make it difficult to deliver more than 72 fighters per year.

In its recent report, the GAO noted that: "Tactical air forces are critical to achieving and maintaining air dominance during combat operations," pointing out that "These aircraft often operate during the first days of a conflict to penetrate enemy air space, defeat air defenses and achieve air dominance."

Only when control of the air has been gained do follow-on ground, air, and naval forces have the necessary freedom to operate within the battle space. Once air dominance is established, tactical aircraft will of course continue to strike ground targets for the remainder of a conflict.

The overall joint force therefore needs the US Air Force to win the air superiority fight, but the highly contested environment presents

a range of challenges for the USAF, putting this at risk. The threat is evolving rapidly, and many scenarios impose difficult payload/range requirements, as well as capability and capacity issues. The US Air Force will need to make concerted efforts if it is to remain the world leader in air superiority capability, using NGAD and F-35 to try to ensure a qualitative edge, and its remaining fourth generation aircraft to solve the capacity/affordability dilemma.

Buried within the facts and figures of the USAF's own *Air and Space Force Magazine 2022 Almanac* is another cause for concern, when it comes to the likely effectiveness of the USAF against a peer threat. The almanac reveals that in 2021, active duty USAF fighter pilots averaged only 6.8 flying training hours per month, while their AFRes colleagues managed just 6.7, and the Guard's fighter pilots little better at 7.3 hours. This may, or may not be enough to maintain competence, but it probably isn't enough to guarantee war-winning, dominance-achieving excellence. As a side note, this author remembers how we all hooted with laughter when we heard that Warsaw Pact pilots were only getting 12 hours per month at the height of the Cold War. It is shocking that USAF fighter pilots are now flying fewer live hours than that. With the increased availability of high fidelity synthetic training devices, there may be no immediate cause for concern, but nor is there room for complacency. ∎

This Lockheed image shows an F-35A toting a notional hypersonic missile. In reality, large weapons are more likely to be carried by the bombers, and by the F-15E and F-15EX. The F-35A compromises its low observability whenever external stores are carried. (Photo: Lockheed Martin)

USAF Fighter Units

The US Air Force has nine major commands (Majcoms) and two Air Reserve Components (ARCs). Air Force Reserve Command counts as both a Majcom and an ARC. Of these, seven operate tactical fast jets (fighters and attack aircraft).

The seven commands of the USAF operating fighters and attack aircraft are Air Combat Command (ACC), Pacific Air Forces (PACAF), United States Air Forces in Europe - Air Forces Africa (USAFE), Air Force Materiel Command (AFMC), Air

Education and Training Command (AETC), Air Force Reserve Command (AFRC) and the Air National Guard (ANG). Only Air Force Global Strike Command (AFGSC), Air Force Special Operations Command (AFSOC) and Air Mobility Command (AFMC) do not do so.

The primary frontline active duty operators of fighters are, of course, Air Combat Command, Pacific Air Forces, and United States Air Forces in Europe - Air Forces Africa, though all are briefly described below.

Air Combat Command

Air Combat Command (ACC), headquartered at Joint Base Langley-Eustis, Virginia, is the primary provider of air combat forces (including combat air, space, and cyberspace power) to America's warfighting commanders. ACC is the successor to Tactical Air Command – having been the lead command for fighter and persistent attack and reconnaissance missions since September 1992.

The Command performs a multitude of missions – as indeed do its fighters and attack aircraft.
ACC is organised under five active duty numbered air forces and the Air Force Warfare Center, with the 15th Air Force responsible for the lion's share of the command's tactical aircraft, which account for 693 of the command's 1,097 assigned aircraft, and for 11 of the command's 28 non-expeditionary wings.
In mid-2022, the command's most numerous tactical aircraft was the F-16, with 168 on charge (149 F-16Cs and 19 F-16Ds). The command also fielded 158 F-15E Strike Eagles, 122 F-35As, 115 A-10As, 107 F-22As and 21 Eagles (18 F-15Cs and three F-15Ds), together with a pair of F-15EX Eagle IIs.

If all of the F-15 variants were to be 'lumped together', the Eagle in its various guises would be the dominant fighter type in the ACC inventory.

15th Air Force

HQ: Shaw Air Force Base, South Carolina
The 15th Air Force, headquartered at Shaw Air Force Base, South Carolina, is responsible for generating and presenting Air Combat Command's conventional forces including

fighters and attack aircraft, as well as remotely piloted aircraft, command and control, and rescue units. In addition to organising, training, and equipping ACC's conventional forces, the 15th AF has a deployable Joint Task Force-capable headquarters that can provide command and control of integrated ACC forces.

1st Fighter Wing, JB Langley-Eustis, VA.
The 1st Fighter Wing, located at Joint Base Langley-Eustis (JBLE), Virginia, operates the F-22A Raptor and T-38 Talon aircraft in the air superiority role.
The 1st Fighter Wing is responsible for one third of the US Air Force's combat-coded F-22 Raptors and is tasked with delivering F-22 air power worldwide to support

Wearing 'FF' tail codes and laden with ferry tanks, a US Air Force F-22 Raptor aircraft assigned to the 1st Fighter Wing taxies out at Joint Base Langley-Eustis, Virginia, on November 3, 2020. (Photo: US Air Force, Nicholas J. De La Pena)

The 20th Fighter Wing Flagship fires an AGM-88 HARM anti-radiation missile. The aircraft wears a fin stripe representing the Wing's three squadrons. (Photo: US Air Force)

Combatant Commander taskings at short notice - providing air superiority for United States or allied forces by engaging and destroying enemy forces, equipment, defences, or installations. The wing operates and maintains two F-22 Air Dominance squadrons, and the F-22 FTU, and also flies the T-38 as a dedicated adversary to increase training capability. The Raptor Formal Training Unit is new to Langley, though the 71st Fighter Training Squadron is not, having previously reactivated in August 2015, flying the Northrop T-38 Talon for adversary training.

The squadron was reactivated as the 71st Fighter Squadron on January 6, 2023, to serve as a formal training unit for the F-22. The unit's first F-22 arrived on March 29, 2023.

The maintainers of the 1st Fighter Wing have set the standard for low observable aircraft maintenance, which is claimed to make the 1st Fighter Wing the most capable and combat ready F-22 wing in the Air Force.

27th Fighter Squadron 'Fighting Eagles': F-22
94th Fighter Squadron 'Hat in the Ring': F-22
71st Fighter Squadron 'Ironmen': F-22 (FTU)

F-22 Raptor Demo Team: F-22
7th Fighter Training Squadron 'Screamin' Demons': T-38

4th Fighter Wing, Seymour Johnson AFB, North Carolina

The 4th Fighter Wing, located at Seymour Johnson AFB, North Carolina, flies F-15E Strike Eagles in support of contingency operations all over the world as part of the Aerospace Expeditionary Force, providing Strike Eagle firepower wherever and whenever it is needed. The Wing's 4th Operations Group had its origins in the Royal Air Force Eagle Squadrons (Nos.71, 121 and 133 Squadrons) transferring to the United States Army Air Forces VIII Fighter Command on September 12, 1942, forming the 4th Fighter Group.

Today, the 4th Fighter Wing has four squadrons equipped with the F-15E.

333rd Fighter Squadron 'Lancers': F-15E formal training unit
334th Fighter Squadron 'Eagles': F-15E
335th Fighter Squadron 'Chiefs': F-15E
336th Fighter Squadron 'Rocketeers': F-15E

20th Fighter Wing, Shaw AFB, South Carolina

The 20th Fighter Wing, located at Shaw AFB, is the air force's largest combat-coded F-16 Fighting Falcon wing. The wing's proud boast is that it provides combat ready airpower and airmen to meet any challenge, anytime, anywhere.

The wing's mission is to provide, project, and sustain combat-ready aircraft in conventional and anti-radiation suppression of enemy air defences (also known as SEAD), strategic attack, counter-air, air interdiction, joint maritime operations, and combat search-and-rescue missions.

The Suppression of Enemy Air Defences is often referred to as the 'Wild Weasel' mission and is typically performed by a pair of fighters. One aircraft allows enemy air defences to target it, enabling the second aircraft to target and destroy the enemy radar. The first aircraft then evades any fired missiles using electronic warfare equipment and skill crafted over countless hours in the cockpit.

55th Fighter Squadron 'Fighting 55th'/'Shooters': F-16CM/DM
77th Fighter Squadron 'Gamblers': F-16CM/DM
79th Fighter Squadron 'Tigers': F-16CM/DM ▶

F-15E Strike Eagles assigned to the 336th Fighter Squadron arrive at Kadena Air Base, Japan, on April 8, 2023. The Strike Eagles arrived from Seymour Johnson Air Force Base, North Carolina, to ensure continuous fighter presence through the phased return of Kadena's fleet of F-15C/D Eagles to the United States. (Photo: US Air Force, Senior Airman Jessi Roth)

Jorge Hernandez-Perez, a 75th Fighter Generation Squadron crew chief, prepares to launch an A-10C Thunderbolt II for a Green Flag-West 23-02 mission at Marine Corps Air Station Miramar, California, on November 9, 2022. (Photo: US Air Force, Senior Airman Zachary Rufus)

23rd Wing 'Flying Tigers' Moody AFB, Georgia

The 23rd Wing, located at Moody AFB, Georgia, operates A-10C Thunderbolt, HC-130J Combat King III and HH-60G Pave Hawk aircraft, and trains to rapidly deploy and execute the Global Precision Attack, Personnel Recovery, and Agile Combat Support service core functions worldwide to meet the requirements of combatant commanders.

The 23d Fighter Group directs the flying operations for the USAF's largest A-10C fighter group, operating in the close air support, forward air control and combat support roles. The group comprises two combat-ready A-10C squadrons and an operations support squadron, with more than 90 pilots and 180 support personnel. There is also one Air Force Reserve associate squadron, operating as part of the 476th Fighter Group.

74th Fighter Squadron 'Flying Tigers': A-10C
75th Fighter Squadron 'Tiger Sharks': A-10C
76th Fighter Squadron (AFRes) 'Vanguards': A-10C

325th FW Tyndall AFB, Florida

The 325th Fighter Wing, located at Tyndall AFB, Florida, sustained a direct hit from Hurricane Michael in 2018. Until then, the wing's primary mission had been to provide air dominance training for F-22 Raptor pilots and other F-22 personnel. The 43rd Fighter Squadron operated as the F-22 FTU, with the 2nd Fighter Training Squadron providing adversary-roled T-38As. From October 11, 2013, the 95th Fighter Squadron was reactivated as an operational F-22 Raptor unit, providing mission-ready air dominance forces in support of the commander, North American Aerospace Defense Command/1st Air Force. It disbanded in 2019, after Hurricane Michael, while the 43rd Fighter Squadron moved to nearby Eglin Air Force Base.

Work is now underway to rebuild Tyndall and shape it to become the air force's first 21st century 'Installation of the Future'. Tyndall plans to welcome F-35 Lightning II aircraft beginning in September 2023.

No based units in spring 2023.

355th Wing Davis-Monthan AFB, Arizona

The 355th Wing is located at Davis-Monthan AFB, Arizona, responsible for training and deploying, employing, and sustaining A-10C Thunderbolt IIs in support of combatant commanders around the globe, primarily to support combat search and rescue and attack missions. Davis-Monthan is also home to EC-130H Compass Calls, HC-130J Combat Kings, HH-60G Pavehawks, a contingent of F-16 Fighting Falcons and some 4,000 stored

Two A-10 Thunderbolt IIs of the 355th Wing fly in formation over southern Arizona, on April 29, 2019. The wing is based at Davis-Monthan Air Force, Arizona. (Photo: US Air Force, SSgt Betty R. Chevalier)

aircraft under the care of the 309th Aerospace Maintenance and Regeneration Group.

Eight A-10s from the 355th Wing were deployed to Bagram Airfield, Afghanistan following the 9/11 attacks. The 355th FW subsequently became the first A-10C unit to deploy to Kandahar Airfield and the first A-10C unit to use the Sniper Advanced Targeting Pod in combat.

354th Fighter Squadron 'Bulldogs': A-10C Thunderbolt II
357th Fighter Squadron 'Dragons': A-10C Thunderbolt II

366th Fighter Wing, Mountain Home AFB, Idaho

The 366th Fighter Wing, located at Mountain Home AFB, Idaho, is home to three fighter squadrons, one of them a Republic of Singapore Air Force unit. The wing also includes the 390th Electronic Combat Squadron at Naval Air Station Whidbey Island, Washington. This squadron is responsible for suppression of enemy air defences in support of expeditionary forces and operates the EA-18G Growler.

Previously a Composite Wing, the 366th Fighter Wing's mission narrowed to a purely fighter role in 2002.

389th Fighter Squadron: F-15E Strike Eagle
391st Fighter Squadron: F-15E Strike Eagle
428th Fighter Squadron, RSAF: F-15SG

388th FW Hill AFB, Utah

The 388th Fighter Wing, located at Hill AFB, Utah, operates some 78 F-35A Lightning

Weapon Systems Officer Capt Lacie Hester returns home after a successful weapons check ride, in her 391st Fighter Squadron F-15E Strike Eagle, on 16 February, 2021. Capt Hester was a 366th Wing WSO whose squadron was temporarily assigned to the 332nd Air Expeditionary Wing, at an undisclosed location somewhere in southwest Asia. (Photo: US Air Force)

II aircraft. The wing's primary mission is to maintain combat readiness to deploy, employ and sustain F-35A Lightning II aircraft worldwide in support of national defence, delivering rapid, decisive air power, anytime, anywhere.

The wing was selected to fly the new F-35 Lightning II fighter in December 2013, and the first to arrive at Hill was unveiled on September 2, 2015, joining the wing's 34th Fighter Squadron. Initial Operating Capability was achieved on August 2, 2016, in accordance with

the directive of the commander of Air Combat Command. The 421st FS was the last Hill-based squadron to fly the F-16, and its final Vipers departed for other wings in September 2017. The 421st Fighter squadron received the wing's 78th and final F-35 in December 2019 and the wing declared 'Full Warfighting Capability' with the F-35A in January 2020.

4th Fighter Squadron, 'Fightin' Fuujins': F-35A
34th Fighter Squadron, 'Rude Rams': F-35A
421st Fighter Squadron, 'Black Widows': F-35A ▶

An F-35A Lightning II lands after an evening sortie at Hill Air Force Base, Utah, on August 19, 2019. The 388th Fighter Wing was the air force's first combat-coded F-35A wing. (Photo: US Air Force, Alex R. Lloyd)

THE FIGHTER FORCE

The 53rd Wing is responsible for test and evaluation, flying a wide range of tactical aircraft. This F-16 was pictured during Exercise Emerald Flag in December 2020.
(Photo: US Air Force, SSgt Joshua Hoskins)

495th Fighter Group, Shaw AFB, South Carolina

The 495th Fighter Group, headquartered at Shaw AFB, was reactivated in 2013 to serve as the headquarters for Air Combat Command's 'active associate' fighter squadrons, integrating active-duty airmen, Air Reserve Component and Air National Guard units to streamline training, spending, and resources. The group included more than 600 active-duty personnel across nine geographically separated fighter squadrons co-located with Air National Guard and Air Reserve host bases.

Components include: the 24th Fighter Squadron 'Leaping Tigers', at Naval Air Station Fort Worth Joint Reserve Base, Texas, an F-16 equipped active associate unit of the 457th Fighter Squadron; the 53rd Fighter Squadron 'Tigers', at Joint Base Andrews, Maryland, an F-16 equipped active associate unit of the 113th Wing's 121st Fighter Squadron; the 315th Fighter Squadron, at Burlington Air National Guard Base, Vermont, an active associate fighter squadron assigned to the 495th Fighter Group and integrated into the 158th Fighter Wing, Vermont Air National Guard; the 316th Fighter Squadron, at McEntire Joint National Guard Base, South Carolina, an F-16 equipped active associate unit of the South Carolina Air National Guard's 169th Fighter Wing – the 'Swamp

Foxes'; the 358th Fighter Squadron 'Lobos', at Whiteman Air Force Base, Missouri, an A-10 equipped active associate unit of the 442nd Fighter Wing; the 367th Fighter Squadron 'Vultures', at Homestead Air Reserve Base, Florida, an F-16 equipped active associate unit of the Air Force Reserve 482nd Fighter Wing; the 377th Fighter Squadron, at Montgomery Air National Guard Base, Alabama, an F-16 equipped active associate unit of the 100th Fighter Squadron of the Alabama Air National Guard's 187th Fighter Wing; and the 383rd Fighter Squadron, at Buckley Space Force Base, Colorado, an F-16 equipped active duty associate unit of the 120th Fighter Squadron.

The 495th Fighter Group also parents the 378th Fighter Squadron, at Truax Field Air National Guard Base, Wisconsin. This is an F-16 equipped active associate unit headquartered out of the 115th Fighter Wing, but with five additional operating locations, which are geographically separated across six Air National Guard Fighter Wings.

These are the 112th Fighter Squadron, part of the 180th Fighter Wing at Toledo Air National Guard Base in Oregon, equipped with the F-16C; the 123rd Fighter Squadron, 142nd Fighter Wing at Portland Air National Guard Base, Oregon, flying the F-15C/D; the F-16 equipped 175th Fighter Squadron, 114th Fighter Wing at Joe Foss Field Air National Guard Station, Sioux Falls, South Dakota; the 176th Fighter Squadron, 115th Fighter Wing flying the F-35A at Truax Field Air National Guard Base, Madison, Wisconsin; the 179th Fighter Squadron, 148th Fighter Wing at Duluth Air National Guard Base, Minnesota, operating

the F-16 Fighting Falcon; and the 194th Fighter Squadron, 144th Fighter Wing at Fresno Air National Guard Base, California operating the F-15C Eagle.

1st Air Force (Air Forces Northern)
HQ: Tyndall AFB, Florida

With its headquarters at Tyndall Air Force Base, near Panama City, Florida, the 1st Air Force is one of four numbered air forces assigned to Air Combat Command. Though it has no assigned tactical aircraft, it is responsible for ensuring the air sovereignty and air defense of the continental United States (CONUS). It provides airspace surveillance and control and directs all air sovereignty activities for the continental United States.

9th Air Force (Air Forces Central)
HQ: Shaw AFB, South Carolina

The 9th Air Force (9AF or AFCENT) is the Air Force Component of United States Central Command (USCENTCOM), a joint Department of Defense unified combatant command responsible for US security interests stretching from the Horn of Africa through the Persian Gulf region, into Central Asia, a 21-nation area of responsibility that includes 17 partner nations in southwest Asia.

The Ninth Air Force (Air Forces Central) parents several air expeditionary wings, of which only the 332nd Air Expeditionary Wing currently operates tactical aircraft types. Tasked with generating, executing, and sustaining combat air power and combat search and rescue forces across the Levant, the 332nd Air Expeditionary Wing operates from officially 'Undisclosed Locations', and includes rotational deployments by 15th Air Force A-10C, F-15E, and F-16C units.

An F-16 Fighting Falcon flown by Major McKay McLaren, a pilot assigned to the 64th Aggressor Squadron, prepares to take off at Nellis Air Force Base, Nevada, prior to a mission on September 11, 2022. (Photo: US Air Force, Senior Airman Zachary Rufus)

ACC Direct Reporting Units

53rd Wing, Eglin AFB, Florida

The 53rd Wing, headquartered at Eglin Air Force Base, reports to the United States Air Force Warfare Center at Nellis AFB, Nevada, which is in turn a direct reporting unit to Headquarters Air Combat Command.

The 53rd Wing manages and executes ACC's operational test and evaluation (OT&E) and tactics development for the A-10, F-15C/E/EX, F-16, F-22, and F-35, and for other ACC types. The unit supports foreign military exploitation and advanced technology demonstrations and manages the evaluation of all air-to-air and air-to-ground weapons, aerial reconnaissance and weapons delivery systems, advanced self-protection systems for combat aircraft, mission planning systems, aircrew flight equipment and life support systems, and agile combat support systems, maintenance equipment and logistics support. The unit aims to "bring the future faster by answering warfighter demands for integrated, multi-domain capabilities."

Several of the 53rd Wing's squadrons operate tactical aircraft types, including the 28th Test and Evaluation Squadron, the 59th Test and Evaluation Squadron, the 85th Test and Evaluation Squadron, and the 422nd Test and Evaluation Squadron.

57th Wing, Nellis AFB, Nevada

The 57th Wing, as the most diverse wing in the air force, provides advanced, realistic, and multi-domain training focused on ensuring dominance through air, space, and cyberspace. The 57th Wing trains innovative leaders and instructors in tactics, training, and high-end warfighting. The Wing has 132 assigned A-10 Thunderbolt II, F-15 Eagle, F-15E Strike Eagle, F-16 Fighting Falcon, F-35A Lightning II, and F-22A Raptor aircraft.

The USAF Weapons School includes a number of squadrons equipped with tactical aircraft types, including the 6th Weapons Squadron (F-35), the 16th WPS (F-16), the 17th WPS (F-15E), the 66th WPS (A-10/JTAC), and the 433rd WPS (F-22).

The Wing also includes the 64th and 65th Aggressor Squadrons, and the USAF Air Demonstration Squadron - The Thunderbirds - all are equipped with the F-16. ➤

An F-35A Lightning II flown by a 65th Aggressor Squadron (AGRS) pilot passes fourth-generation F-16 Fighting Falcons assigned to the 64 AGRS at Nellis Air Force Base, Nevada on May 26, 2022. (Photo: US Air Force, A1C Josey Blades)

Pacific Air Forces

Pacific Air Forces (PACAF), headquartered at Joint Base Pearl Harbor-Hickam, Hawaii, is the Air Component that supports United States Indo-Pacific Command (USINDOPACOM), while integrating air, space, and cyberspace capabilities.

PACAF is agile, resilient, and lethal, and, in co-ordination with other components, allies, and partners, provides USINDOPACOM with integrated expeditionary air force capabilities, including strike, air mobility, and rescue forces in order to ensure regional stability and security and safeguard a free and open Indo-Pacific.

PACAF consists of three numbered air forces and ten bases, and as at mid-2022, included some 209 tactical aircraft. This total included 135 F-16s (123 F-16Cs and 12 F-16Ds), 54 F-22s, 53 F-15C/Ds, 43 F-35As and 24 A-10Cs. Since then, the PACAF-based F-15s have been withdrawn, replaced by rotational shorter-term deployments by F-16s and F-35s.

5th Air Force

HQ: Yokota AB, Japan
The 5th Air Force, known as the Fighting Fifth, headquartered at Yokota Air Base, Japan, is the US Air Force's oldest continuously serving numbered air force. It has provided more than 75 years of continuous air power to the Pacific

US Air Force Capt Derek Kear, a 67th Fighter Squadron F-15C Eagle pilot, performs visual checks during aircraft launch procedures at Kadena Air Base, Japan, on October 26, 2021. Kadena's F-15 fighter squadrons were progressively returning their aircraft to storage and to other units as this bookazine was being produced. (Photo: US Air Force, Senior Airman Jessi Monte)

US Air Force Col Jesse J. Friedel, 35th Fighter Wing commander, steps out of an F-16 Fighting Falcon cockpit after his fini-flight at Misawa Air Base, Japan, on June 22, 2022. The Wing's F-16s wear WW (Wild Weasel) tail codes. (Photo: US Air Force, A1C Leon Redfern)

An 80th Fighter Squadron F-16D Fighting Falcon, wearing the WP tail codes of the 8th Fighter Wing, flies from Kwangju Air Base, Republic of Korea during exercise Max Thunder 10-02. (US Air Force, Master Sgt Jason Wilkerson)

since its establishment in September 1941, and is tasked with defending Japan, responding to regional contingencies, and enhancing the longstanding US-Japanese Security Alliance. In partnership with Japan's own forces, the 5th Air Force is positioned to deter aggression and maintain regional stability. It has three main bases but only one of these has permanently based fighters.

18th Wing, Kadena, Japan
The withdrawal of F-15 Eagles from the 18th Wing began on December 1, 2022, and the 18th Wing hosted the Kadena Eagle Sunset Celebration, from April 14-15. The phased withdrawal of the F-15C from Kadena saw the disbandment of the 44th Fighter Squadron 'Vampire Bats' and the 67th Fighter Squadron 'Fighting Cocks'. To 'plug the gap', F-35A Lightning IIs from the Eielson-based 355th Fighter Squadron arrived at Kadena Air Base, on March 28, 2023.

35th FW Misawa AB, Japan
The 35th Fighter Wing is headquartered at Misawa Air Base on the shores of Lake Ogawara in Misawa City in the Aomori Prefecture. Misawa is the northernmost US base in Japan and is a bilateral, joint-service, civilian-use air base in the Pacific.

The 35th Fighter Wing is tasked with providing "worldwide deployable forces, protecting US interests in the Pacific and defending Japan

with sustained forward presence and focused mission support."

The wing operates and maintains two squadrons of Block 50 F-16CM and DM Fighting Falcons. The 35th Fighter Wing specialises in the suppression and destruction of enemy air defences and claims to be the USAF's premier Wild Weasel organisation.

13th Fighter Squadron 'The Panther Pack': F-16CM/DM
14th Fighter Squadron: F-16CM/DM

7th Air Force
HQ: Osan AB, South Korea
The mission of 7th Air Force is to deter, protect and defend the Republic of Korea from attack by North Korea and maintain the armistice. 7th Air Force provides what it calls "ready to fight tonight air power - precise, intense, and overwhelming; whenever and wherever needed." The 7th AF maintains fighter wings at Kunsan and Osan and plans and directs air component operations in the Republic of Korea and in the Northwest Pacific in support of US Pacific Command, United Nations Command, US-ROK Combined Forces Command and US Forces Korea.

8th Fighter Wing 'Wolf Pack', Kunsan AB, South Korea
The 8th Fighter Wing's mission is to "Defend the Base, Accept Follow-On Forces, and Take

the Fight North!" For this, the Wing fields two F-16 squadrons, which began to re-equip with aircraft upgraded with AN/APG-83 radar under the POBIT project with the arrival of Wolf Pack Tail 021, which re-joined the 8th Fighter Wing's pack on April 4, 2023.

It was said that: "The modernisation effort will improve the USAF's ability to safeguard a free and open Indo-Pacific region and the stability of the Korean Peninsula."

Colonel John D. Caldwell, 8 FW vice commander, who flew the upgraded aircraft back to Kunsan, said: "With regards to the Wolf Pack's 'Take the Fight North' mission, these upgrades primarily allow us to keep pace with near-peer threats, but also have a large hand in the deterrence mission. It will definitely be a part of the decision calculus for the Democratic People's Republic of Korea (DPRK), because the more lethal and survivable we can make our forces here on the peninsula, the more likely we are to deter aggression. The goal is to present a force so capable, that [the DPRK] decides, instead of pulling a trigger, to pick up the phone to talk. Of course, if deterrence breaks down, the modernisation programme will significantly improve our ability to defend South Korea and take the fight north if necessary."

35th Fighter Squadron 'Pantons'/'Cyclones Flying Circus': F-16CM/DM
80th Fighter Squadron 'Headhunters'/'Juvats': F-16CM/DM ▷

51st Fighter Wing 'Mustangs', Osan AB, South Korea

The 51st Fighter Wing is based at Osan Air Base, just 48 miles south of the Korean DMZ, making it the most forward deployed permanently based wing in the air force. The wing has been based entirely in the Far East during its entire existence, most notably as the 51st Fighter-Interceptor Wing during the Korean War. Today the wing is charged with providing mission ready airmen to execute combat operations and to receive follow-on forces, its F-16 and A-10 Squadrons conducting the full spectrum of missions while providing for the defence of the Republic of Korea.

25th Fighter Squadron 'Assam Draggins' : A-10C/OA-10C
36th Fighter Squadron 'The Flying Fiends': Block 40 F-16CM/DM

11th Air Force

HQ: JB Elmendorf-Richardson, Alaska

During the early 1990s the mission of the 11th Air Force shifted from one of defending Alaska against the Soviet bomber threat to one of supporting worldwide deployment, meeting regional contingencies and of providing training opportunities for other units. The 11th Air Force supports the vital Pacific air bridge operation enabling the strategic movement of contingency forces during crisis response. It provides support to federal and state authorities during civil emergencies, search and rescue operations and counter-narcotics interdictions.

The 11th still provides combat ready forces for COMPACAF, and defends Alaska, Hawaii, Guam, and key strategic nodes against all threats.

3rd Wing, JB Elmendorf-Richardson, Alaska

The 3rd Wing is the largest and principal unit within the 11th Air Force. It is stationed at Joint Base Elmendorf-Richardson, Alaska. The 3rd Wing trains and equips an Air Expeditionary Force lead wing composed of F-22A, E-3G,

Wearing AK tail codes, an F-22A Raptor assigned to the 3rd Wing's 525th Fighter Squadron flies with Philippine Air Force FA-50PH's over the South China Sea, on March 14, 2023. (Photo: US Air Force, Senior Airman Jessi Roth)

An A-10C Thunderbolt II, assigned to the 25th Fighter Squadron, takes off during a routine training event at Osan Air Base, Republic of Korea, on January 30, 2023. The 51st Fighter Wing uses a black and white chequerboard as its unit marking. (Photo: US Air Force, A1C Aaron Edwards)

and C-17 aircraft, providing air supremacy, surveillance, worldwide airlift, and agile combat support forces which together project power and reach. The wing has two F-22 Squadrons, while the 302nd Fighter Squadron is part of the Air Force Reserve Command's 477th Fighter Group at Elmendorf. In August 2022, 12 of the 90th Fighter Squadron's F-22 Raptors deployed to Łask Air Base, Poland as part of NATO's air shielding mission.

90th Fighter Squadron 'The Dicemen': F-22A
525th Fighter Squadron 'The Bulldogs': F-22A
302nd Fighter Squadron: F-22A

15th Wing - Hickam Air Force Base, Hawaii

The 15th Wing at Joint Base Pearl Harbor–Hickam, Hawaii, reports to the 11th Air Force at Elmendorf, 2,800 miles north! Its mission is to enhance PACAF's power and reach by ensuring world-class en route support and maintaining operationally ready forces which also support the Hawaiian Air National Guard. The 19th Fighter Squadron is an active duty associate unit of the Hawaii Air National Guard's 199th Fighter Squadron (154th Wing), as part of the air force's total force initiative.

19th Fighter Squadron 'Gamecocks': F-22

354th Fighter Wing, Eielson AFB, Alaska

The 354th Fighter Wing is the host unit at Eielson Air Force Base, some 26 miles southeast of Fairbanks, Alaska. The 354th Fighter Wing's mission is to provide "USINDOPACOM combat-ready airpower,

advanced integration training, and a strategic arctic basing option."

355th Fighter Squadron 'Fighting Falcons': F-35A
356th Fighter Squadron 'Green Demons': F-35A
18th Aggressor Squadron 'Blue Foxes': F-16C/D ➤

A US Air Force F-35A Lightning II assigned to the 356th Fighter Squadron at Eielson Air Force Base, Alaska, lands at Andersen AFB, Guam, as part of Cope North on 21 February 6, 2021. (Photo: US Air Force, Senior Airman Jonathan Valdes Montijo)

US Air Forces in Europe – Air Forces Africa (USAFE-AFAFRICA)

Headquartered at Ramstein AB, Germany, USAFE-AFAFRICA is the air component for both US European Command and US Africa Command, with an area of operations spanning three continents, 104 independent nations and covering more than 19 million square miles.

USAFE-AFAFRICA controls eight wings based in Europe (three of them equipped with fighter aircraft), plus 83 geographically separated units and exercises administrative control over the US personnel assigned to the Heavy Airlift Wing at Papa AB, Hungary. There are no US air forces permanently based in Africa, but the command provides expeditionary base support, force protection, construction, and resupply operations in austere locations. The command's mission is to defend vital US interests, deter aggression, and deepen relationships with Allies and partners by projecting combat-ready, forward-based, and deployed airpower in Europe and Africa. Fighter strength in mid-2022 included 78 F-16C/Ds (four of them D models), 55 F-15Es and 20 F-15C/Ds (two of them two-seaters). Since then, the F-15C/Ds have been withdrawn and replaced by a similar number of F-35As, and more Joint Strike Fighters are expected.

3rd Air Force
HQ: Ramstein AB, Germany
The 3rd Air Force is the only numbered air force in US Air Forces in Europe and Air Forces Africa, with ten wings across two continents stretching from the Arctic to the Cape of Good Hope. Through the NATO Partnership for Peace programme, the headquarters manages military contact and assistance programs for a number of countries in Eastern Europe. The 3rd Air Force is also responsible for contingency planning and support of American security interests in Africa. The 3rd Air Force also oversees host nation support agreements for all US military forces based in the United Kingdom through the command's 3 AF-UK headquarters at RAF Mildenhall. The 3rd Air Force includes three fighter wings.

31st Fighter Wing, Aviano AB, Italy
The 31st Fighter Wing is the only US fighter wing south of the Alps. This strategic location makes the wing critical to operations in NATO's southern region. The mission of the 31st Fighter Wing is deterrence, and to: "Win the current fight and be ready to win the next fight." The wing has recently focused on further improving its Agile Combat Employment (ACE) capabilities, and maintains two F-16 fighter squadrons, the 555th Fighter Squadron and the 510th Fighter Squadron, capable of conducting offensive and defensive air combat operations.

510th Fighter Squadron 'Buzzards': F-16CM/DM
555th Fighter Squadron 'Triple Nickel':
  F-16CM/DM

A US Air Force F-16 Fighting Falcon from the 510th Fighter Squadron (part of the 31st Fighter Wing) takes off from Aviano Air Base, Italy, on March 16, 2020. (Photo: US Air Force, A1C Ericka A. Woolever)

Two F-15E Strike Eagles and an F-15C Eagle assigned to the 48th Fighter Wing painted with their respective squadron heritage colour schemes fly over southern England on September 3, 2019. The Liberty Wing now includes two F-35A squadrons and two Strike Eagle units. (Photo: US Air Force, Tech Sgt Matthew Plew)

48th 'Liberty' Fighter Wing, RAF Lakenheath, UK

The 'Liberty Wing' is the US Air Forces in Europe's only fourth and fifth-generation fighter wing, and provides all-weather, day or night air superiority and air-to-ground precision combat capability. The 48th FW has formed the foundation of USAFE's combat capability for many years and has played a key role in anti-terrorism operations since September 11, 2001, as well as flying combat missions and providing combat support in Operations Enduring Freedom and Iraqi Freedom.

492nd Fighter Squadron 'Bolars'/'Madhatters': F-15E
493rd Fighter Squadron 'Grim Reapers': F-35A
494th Fighter Squadron 'Panthers': F-15E
495th Fighter Squadron 'Valkyries': F-35A

52nd Fighter Wing, Spangdahlem AB, Germany

The 52nd Fighter Wing maintains, deploys, and employs F-16CM Fighting Falcons in support of NATO and US national defence directives - providing air power options aimed at deterring and if necessary, combatting aggression. The unit is tasked with air interdiction and counter air operations and is EUCOM's sole 'Wild Weasel' squadron. It is the only remaining wing based in Germany – which once also hosted tactical fighter and reconnaissance wings at Bitburg, Hahn, Ramstein, and Sembach. The 52nd Fighter Wing includes only a single F-16 squadron and this unit is sometimes thinly spread, having deployed aircraft to Łask AB, Poland and to Fetesti Air Base, Romania.

480th Fighter Squadron 'Warhawks': F-16CM/DM

A US Air Force F-16 Fighting Falcon aircraft from the 480th Fighter Squadron at Spangdahlem Air Base, Germany, lands in Romania, on February 11, 2022. 52nd Fighter Wing units routinely train for rapid response operations, keeping airmen, equipment, and capabilities ready for any contingency. (Photo: US Air Force, Senior Airman Ali Stewart)

Air Education and Training Command (AETC)

Headquartered at Joint Base San Antonio, Randolph, Texas, Air Education and Training Command (AETC) is the USAF's primary training and professional education command.

Air Education and Training Command (AETC) is a huge organisation, with 48,000 active duty and Air Reserve Component members, 14,000 civilian personnel, and approximately 1,600 aircraft. Within this total AETC has more tactical fighters than USAFE-AFAFRICA, with some 249 aircraft in two fighter wings! In mid-2022, these included 83 F-16Cs and 51 F-16Ds and 115 F-35As.

After completing the primary phase of SUPT and ENJJPT, student pilots qualified for fighter or bomber assignments are assigned to the fighter/bomber track and train in the T-38 Talon at the SUPT and ENJJPT bases. For those destined for fighter aircraft, an Introduction to Fighter Fundamentals (IFF) course, is undertaken at Randolph AFB, Texas, Columbus AFB, Mississippi, or Sheppard AFB, Texas on the T-38.

AETC has six Formal Training Units (FTUs), including an AETC-gained fighter wing of the Oregon Air National Guard at Kingsley Field for the F-15.

F-16 Fighting Falcon training is undertaken at Holloman AFB, Arizona by an AETC fighter group formerly controlled from Luke AFB. There is also an AETC-gained fighter wing of the Texas Air National Guard at Lackland AFB/Kelly Field, and an AETC-gained fighter wing of the Arizona Air National Guard at Tucson Air National Guard Base, focusing on international (NATO/Allied/Coalition) pilot training in support of the F-16 Foreign Military Sales (FMS) programme. F-35 Lightning II training is undertaken at Eglin AFB, Florida and Luke AFB, Arizona.

19th Air Force

HQ: JBSA-Randolph, Texas

The 19th Air Force was re-activated on July 1, 1993 as part of the new Air Education and Training Command (AETC). It was assigned to Randolph AFB, Texas and has the mission of conducting AETC's flying training.

The AETC-gained ANG and AFRC units are listed under those commands.

33rd Fighter Wing ('Nomads') Eglin AFB, Florida

The 33rd Fighter Wing is assigned to Air Education and Training Command's 19th Air Force and is stationed at Eglin Air Force Base, Florida as a tenant unit. Its main mission is to train United States Air Force and partner nation pilots and maintainers on the Lockheed Martin F-35 Lightning II. USMC F-35B training ended in 2014, and USN F-35C training in 2019.

58th Fighter Squadron 'Gorillas': F-35A
60th Fighter Squadron: F-35A

49th Fighter Wing, Holloman AFB, New Mexico

The 49th Wing of Air Education and Training Command at Holloman Air Force Base, New Mexico includes the 54th Fighter Group, which operates as an F-16 Fighting Falcon training unit, with three assigned squadrons.

8th Fighter Squadron 'The Black Sheep': F-16C/D

A US Air Force Airman 1st Class David Burgner, an avionics technician with the 60th Aircraft Maintenance Unit, 33rd Fighter Wing, prepares an F-35A Lightning II for take-off at Naval Air Station Key West, Florida, on February 13, 2023. Airmen with the 33rd Fighter Wing travelled to NAS Key West to conduct off-site training while avoiding delays due to inclement weather conditions. (Photo: US Air Force, Airmen Christian Corley)

311th Fighter Squadron 'Sidewinders': F-16C/D
314th Fighter Squadron 'Warhawks': F-16C/D

56th Fighter Wing 'Thunderbolts', Luke AFB, Arizona

The 56th Fighter Wing is the world's largest Lockheed Martin F-35 Lightning II wing and one of two US Air Force F-35 training units. It still has a residual F-16 training role, especially for some FMS customers – notably Singapore and Taiwan – the latter operating from Morris Air National Guard Base, Tucson ANGB. The 56th also parents the 550th Fighter Squadron, a Total Force Integration unit co-located at Kingsley Field with the 173rd Fighter Wing (Oregon ANG).

21st Fighter Squadron 'The Gamblers' - Block 20 F-16A/B
61st Fighter Squadron 'Top Dogs': F-35A
62nd Fighter Squadron 'Spikes': F-35A
63rd Fighter Squadron 'Panthers': F-35A
308th Fighter Squadron 'Emerald Knights': F-35A
309th Fighter Squadron 'Wild Ducks': F-16C/D
310th Fighter Squadron 'Top Hats': Converting from F-16 to F-35A
425th Fighter Squadron 'Black Widows': F-16C/D RSAF
550th Fighter Squadron 'Silver Eagles': F-15C/D

The 49th Wing Flagship, operating from Holloman Air Force Base, fires an AIM-9M at WSEP East on March 10, 2021. (Photo: US Air Force, 1st Lt Savanah Bray)

Air Force Materiel Command (AFMC)

Headquartered at Wright-Patterson AFB, Ohio, AFMC is tasked with the research, development, procurement, testing, and sustainment of USAF weapon systems.

Air Force Materiel Command (AFMC) does operate small numbers of tactical fighter aircraft types in order to conduct its research and testing roles.

Its fleet includes 22 F-16Ds, 12 single-seat F-16Cs, five F-15Es, four F-22s, and pairs of A-10Cs, F-15Cs, and F-35As. Its units include the Air Force Test Center (AFTC)

at Edwards AFB, California, the 96th Test Wing at Eglin AFB, Florida, and the 412th Test Wing and US Air Force Test Pilot School at Edwards AFB, California. ➤

56th Fighter Wing F-16 Fighting Falcons return to their base at Luke Air Force Base, Arizona after a successful mission on September 14, 2010. (Photo: US Air Force, Jim Hanseltine)

Air Force Reserve Command (AFRC)

Headquartered at Robins AFB, Georgia, the Air Force Reserve has three numbered air forces, though only one of these operates fighters.

With the adoption of the Total Force Policy in August 1970, the Robins AFB located Air Force Reserve became a multi-mission force, flying the same modern aircraft types as the active air force, and held to the same readiness standards and inspections as corresponding active duty units. AFRC has approximately 450 aircraft of its own, operating 55 A-10C, 52 F-16C and two F-16D aircraft in standalone AFRC fighter wings that are operationally aligned with Air Combat Command (ACC).

AFRC also has access to several hundred additional active duty USAF aircraft via AFRC 'Associate' wings that are co-located with active duty air force wings, sharing access to those same active duty air force aircraft, including Air Combat Command F-22A Raptor air dominance fighters, F-16 Fighting Falcon and F-15E Strike Eagle multi-role fighters, and A-10 Thunderbolt II ground attack aircraft. These are jointly operated by active duty ACC personnel and AFRC aircrews in Associate units.

Under the Associate Reserve programme active duty, Air Force Reserve and Air National Guard members combine forces and missions using the 'Total Force' integration concept, with the reserve components providing manpower to complement the Total Force. Reserve units are paired with an active-duty unit and share a single set of aircraft.

In a traditional associate unit, air force reservists fly and maintain aircraft owned by the active duty regular air force unit (typically a wing level organisation), with an Air Force Reserve or Air National Guard associate unit being co-located with the active duty unit, providing only manpower.

In an active associate unit, the Air Force Reserve or Air National Guard unit 'owns' the aircraft, while the active duty regular air force provides air crews, aircraft maintenance and support personnel who share the responsibility for flying and maintaining the AFRC or ANG-owned aircraft. Both approaches result in a more cost-effective way to meet mission requirements.

10th Air Force

HQ: Naval Air Station Fort Worth Joint Reserve Base/Carswell Field, Texas

The 10th Air Force is the AFRC numbered air force whose units and aircraft are primarily gained by the Combat Air Forces (CAF), including Air Combat Command (ACC), Air Force Global Strike Command (AFGSC), Pacific Air Forces (PACAF), and Air Education and Training Command (AETC).

44th Fighter Group, Eglin Air Force Base, Florida

The 44th Fighter Group is an associate unit of the active duty 325th Fighter Wing. The Group's 301st Fighter Squadron flies the F-22 Raptor. The unit moved to Eglin following hurricane damage to its former base at Tyndall. If mobilised to active duty, the 44th FG would be operationally gained by ACC. Otherwise, it functions as a geographically separated unit (GSU) of AFRC's F-16 equipped 301st Fighter Wing at NAS JRB Fort Worth, Texas.

301st Fighter Squadron, AFRC: F-22A

301st Fighter Wing, Naval Air Station Fort Worth Joint Reserve Base/Carswell Field, Texas

A large single-squadron wing, with 32 F-16s (having gained aircraft from Hill AFB and the Virginia Air National Guard, the 301st Fighter Wing is expected to re-equip with 24 PAA (Primary Aircraft Authorised) and two BAI (Backup Aircraft Inventory) F-35As in 2024. If mobilised, Air Combat Command would gain the wing.

457th Fighter Squadron 'Spads': F-16C/D

414th Fighter Group, Seymour Johnson Air Force Base, North Carolina

The 414th Fighter Group is an associate unit of the active duty 4th Fighter Wing. If mobilised the wing would be gained by ACC but is otherwise assigned to the 944th Fighter Wing of Air Force Reserve Command, stationed alongside the 4th at Seymour Johnson Air Force Base, North Carolina, and similarly equipped with the Strike Eagle.

307th Fighter Squadron 'Stingers': F-15E

419th Fighter Wing, Hill AFB, Utah

The 419th FW is an associate unit of the Active Duty 388th Fighter Wing, Air Combat Command (ACC), and if mobilised the wing would be gained by ACC. The wing's designated flying squadron is the 466th Fighter Squadron, which is currently the only combat-coded Reserve F-35 unit.

466th Fighter Squadron 'Diamondbacks': F-35A

442nd Fighter Wing, Whiteman Air Force Base, Missouri

The 442nd Fighter Wing is an Air Reserve Component of the United States Air Force. It is assigned to 10th Air Force, Air Force Reserve Command, stationed at Whiteman Air Force Base, Missouri. The wing trains reserve personnel and the 358th Fighter Squadron to operate, maintain and support the Fairchild Republic A-10 Thunderbolt II at combat readiness. The wing's 476th Fighter Group

Major Brett Gedman of the 301st Fighter Squadron, takes off in an F-22A Raptor while wearing the Next Generation Fixed Wing Helmet (NGFWH) on March 24, 2023, at Eglin Air Force Base, Florida. (Photo: US Air Force, Samuel King Jr.)

An A-10 Thunderbolt II, assigned to Whiteman Air Force Base, taxis down the flight line at Kandahar Airfield, Afghanistan, on January 19, 2018, during operations in support of the Resolute Support Mission and Operation Freedom's Sentinel. (Photo: US Air Force, SSgt Sean Martin)

supports the 23rd Wing at Moody Air Force Base, Georgia.

303rd Fighter Squadron 'KC Hawgs': A-10C
358th Fighter Squadron 'Lobos': A-10C

477th Fighter Group, Joint Base Elmendorf-Richardson, Alaska

The 477th Fighter Group is an AFRC Associate unit within the Active Duty 3rd Wing, and is operationally gained by Pacific Air Forces. The 477th FG is a classic associate: An active duty (Regular) component unit retains principal responsibility for the weapons system, which it shares with reserve component units, with separate organisational structures and chains-of-command. The group is Air Force Reserve Command's first F-22A Raptor unit, and is responsible for recruiting, training, developing, and retaining reserve citizen airmen to support 3rd Wing and Expeditionary Air Force mission requirements.

The men and women of the 477th FG are integrated with their active duty air force partners in most F-22A mission areas increasing efficiency and overall combat capability while retaining reserve administrative support and career enhancement.

302nd Fighter Squadron: F-22

482nd Fighter Wing, Homestead Air Reserve Base, Florida

The 482nd Fighter Wing is an Air Force Component (ARC) unit of the 10th Air Force, Air Force Reserve Command, stationed at Homestead Air Reserve Base, Florida. If mobilised to active duty, the 482nd FW would be operationally gained by Air Combat Command (ACC). It is a combat coded unit which provides F-16C and F-16D (Block 30) Fighting Falcon multirole fighter aircraft, along with mission ready pilots and support personnel, for short-notice worldwide deployment. The 482nd FW is home to the 367th Fighter Squadron (367 FS), an active duty regular air force F-16 unit assigned to ACC but integrating with the 482nd FW under the Total Force Integration (TFI) concept.

93rd Fighter Squadron 'The Makos': F-16C/D
367th Fighter Squadron 'Vultures': F-16C/D
(Active Associate)

Colonel Gina 'Torch' Sabric, commander of the 419th Fighter Wing at Hill Air Force Base, Utah, was the Air Force Reserve's first female F-35 pilot. (Photo: US Air Force, Todd Cromar)

926th Wing (classic associate) Nellis AFB, Nevada

The 926th Wing is an Air Force Reserve unit based at Nellis Air Force Base, as an associate reserve unit integrated with units from a number of commands.

The wing's reservists are integrated into a number of regular air force units, conducting combat operations, operational test and evaluation, tactics development, and advanced training. It also supports the US Air Force's first remotely piloted aircraft wing, the 432nd WG/432nd AEW, equipped with the MQ-1 Predator and MQ-9 Reaper unmanned aircraft.

The wing's tactical aircraft squadrons include units supporting the 53rd and 57th Wings. The 706th Fighter Squadron oversees Air Force Reserve Command fighter pilots supporting the United States Air Force Warfare Center as an associate of the 57th Wing. Pilots assigned to the 706th fly the F-16 Fighting Falcon, F-15 Eagle, F-15E Strike Eagle, F-22 Raptor and F-35 Lightning II, as well as the A-10 Thunderbolt II.

84th Test and Evaluation Squadron: Various types
706th Fighter Squadron: Various types

944th Fighter Wing, Luke AFB, Arizona

The 944th Fighter Wing is an Air Reserve component of the United States Air Force. It is an associate unit of the 56th Fighter Wing of Air Education and Training Command (AETC) and if mobilised the wing would be gained by AETC. It has two GSUs (Geographically Separated Units) – the 924th Fighter Group at Davis-Monthan Air Force Base, Arizona and the 414th Fighter Group at Seymour Johnson Air Force Base, North Carolina, in addition to the 944th Operations Group at Luke.

47th Fighter Squadron 'Dogpatchers': A-10C (Davis-Monthan AFB)
52nd Fighter Squadron 'Ninjas': F-35A (Luke AFB)
69th Fighter Squadron 'Werewolves': F-16C/D (Luke AFB)
307th Fighter Squadron 'Stingers': F-15E (Seymour Johnson AFB)

>

Air National Guard (ANG)

The Air National Guard is a federal military reserve force of the United States Air Force, forming the 'air militia' of the 50 US states, as well as the District of Columbia, the Commonwealth of Puerto Rico, and the territories of Guam and the US Virgin Islands.

When operating under the jurisdiction of the state governor, under Title 32 of the United States Code, Air National Guard units fulfil their militia role. However, if federalised under Title 10 (by order of the President of the United States), Air National Guard units form an active part of the United States Air Force and are operationally gained by an active duty air force major command (MAJCOM).

The vast majority of ANG units are gained by either ACC (or AMC in the case of airlift units), though a handful are operationally gained by Pacific Air Forces (PACAF), and by Air Education and Training Command (AETC).

ANG units are jointly administered by the states and the National Guard Bureau, a joint bureau of the US Army and US Air Force that oversees the United States National Guard.

Each ANG wing will either have its own assigned aircraft or will share aircraft from an active duty air force or the air force reserve unit under an 'associate' arrangement. Air National Guard activities may be located on active duty air force bases, air reserve bases, naval air stations/joint reserve bases, or air national guard bases and stations - which may be tenants on civilian-controlled joint civil-military airports.

ANG fighter units are assigned to these State National Guards: Alabama Air National Guard (187th Fighter Wing), Arizona Air National Guard (162nd Fighter Wing), California Air National Guard (144th Fighter Wing), Colorado Air National Guard (140th Wing), Florida Air National Guard (125th Fighter Wing), Hawaii Air National Guard (154th Wing), Idaho Air National Guard (124th Fighter Wing), Illinois Air National Guard (183rd Fighter Wing), Indiana Air National Guard (122nd Fighter Wing), Louisiana Air National Guard (159th Fighter Wing), Maryland Air National Guard (175th Wing), Massachusetts Air National Guard (104th Fighter Wing), Michigan Air National Guard (127th Wing), Minnesota Air National Guard (148th Fighter Wing), New Jersey Air National Guard (177th Fighter Wing), Ohio Air National Guard (180th Fighter Wing), Oklahoma Air National Guard (138th Fighter Wing), Oregon Air National Guard (142nd Fighter Wing and 173rd Fighter Wing), South Carolina Air National Guard (169th Fighter Wing), South Dakota Air National Guard (114th Fighter Wing), Texas Air National Guard (149th Fighter Wing), Vermont Air National Guard (158th Fighter Wing), Virginia Air National Guard (192nd Fighter Wing), Wisconsin Air National Guard (115th Fighter Wing), and the District of Columbia Air National Guard (113th Wing).

104th Fighter Wing, Massachusetts Air National Guard, Barnes ANGB
131st Fighter Squadron 'Barnstormers': F-15C/D

113th Wing, District of Columbia Air National Guard, Joint Base Andrews (former Andrews AFB), Maryland
121st Fighter Squadron 'Capital Guardians': F-16C/D

114th Fighter Wing, South Dakota Air National Guard, Joe Foss Field ANGS, Sioux Falls
175th Fighter Squadron 'Fightin' Lobos': F-16C/D

115th Fighter Wing, Wisconsin Air National Guard, Truax Field ANGB
176th Fighter Squadron 'Badger Air Militia': F-16C/D

122nd Fighter Wing, Indiana Air National Guard, Fort Wayne ANGS
163rd Fighter Squadron 'Blacksnakes': A-10C

124th Fighter Wing, Idaho Air National Guard, Gowen Field ANGB
190th Fighter Squadron 'Skullbangers': A-10C

125th Fighter Wing, Florida Air National Guard, Jacksonville ANGB
159th Fighter Squadron 'Boxin' Gators': F-15C/D
125th Fighter Wing, Detachment 1, Homestead ARB (former Homestead AFB)

127th Wing, Michigan Air National Guard, Selfridge ANGB (former Selfridge AFB)
107th Fighter Squadron 'The Red Devils': A-10C

138th Fighter Wing, Oklahoma Air National Guard, Tulsa ANGB
125th Fighter Squadron 'Tulsa Vipers': F-16C/D
138th Fighter Wing, Detachment 1 (Alert Det), Ellington Field JRB, Texas

An F-35A Lightning II aircraft piloted by US Air Force Lt Col Michael Koob arrives at Truax Field in Madison, Wisconsin on April 25, 2023. The aircraft was one of the first three F-35s to arrive on the base following the air force's decision to assign the fifth-generation fighters to the 115th Fighter Wing in April 2020. (Photo: US Air National Guard, Isabella Jansen)

140th Wing, Colorado Air National Guard, Buckley Space Force Base
  120th Fighter Squadron 'Mile High Militia': F-16C/D

142nd Fighter Wing, Oregon Air National Guard, Portland ANGB
  123rd Fighter Squadron 'Redhawks': F-15C/D

144th Fighter Wing, California Air National Guard, Fresno Air National Guard Base
  194th Fighter Squadron 'Griffins': F-15C/D
  144th Fighter Wing Alert Detachment, March ARB (former March AFB)

148th Fighter Wing, Minnesota Air National Guard, Duluth ANGB
  179th Fighter Squadron 'Bulldogs': F-16C/D

149th Fighter Wing, Texas Air National Guard, Lackland AFB/Kelly Field Annex (former Kelly AFB) (AETC gained)
  182nd Fighter Squadron 'Gunfighters': F-16C/D

154th Wing, Hawaii Air National Guard, Hickam AFB (PACAF gained)
  199th Fighter Squadron: 'Mytai Fighters': F-22

158th Fighter Wing, Vermont Air National Guard, Burlington ANGB (former Ethan Allen AFB)
  134th Fighter Squadron 'The Green Mountain Boys': F-35A

159th Fighter Wing, Louisiana Air National Guard, NAS JRB New Orleans
  122nd Fighter Squadron 'Bayou Militia': F-15C/D

162nd Fighter Wing, Arizona Air National Guard, Tucson ANGB (AETC gained)
  148th Fighter Squadron 'Kickin' Ass': F-16C/D
  152nd Fighter Squadron 'Tigers': F-16C/D

A black and grey US Air Force A-10 Thunderbolt II from the Indiana Air National Guard's 122nd Fighter Wing 'Blacksnakes', painted at the Air National Guard paint facility in Sioux City, Iowa on July 2, 2021. In a departure from the standard A-10 two-tone grey, the paint scheme was created by request in order to commemorate the 100th anniversary of aviation in the Indiana National Guard. (Photo: US Air National Guard)

  195th Fighter Squadron: 'Warhawks' F-16C/D
  Air National Guard Air Force Reserve Command Test Center: F-16C/D Block 25/32

169th Fighter Wing, South Carolina Air National Guard, McEntire ANGB
  157th Fighter Squadron: 'Swamp Foxes': F-16C/D
  316th Fighter Squadron: F-16C/D (Active Associate)

173rd Fighter Wing, Oregon Air National Guard, Kingsley Field ANGB
  114th Fighter Squadron 'Eager Beavers': F-15C/D FTU

175th Wing, Maryland Air National Guard, Martin State Airport/Warfield ANGB
  104th Fighter Squadron 'Fightin' Os': A-10C

177th Fighter Wing 'Jersey Devils', New Jersey Air National Guard, Atlantic City ANGB
  119th Fighter Squadron: F-16C/D

180th Fighter Wing, Ohio Air National Guard, Toledo ANGB
  112th Fighter Squadron 'Stingers': F-16C/D

183rd Fighter Wing, Illinois Air National Guard, Capital Airport ANGS
  170th Fighter Squadron: F-16C/D

187th Fighter Wing, Alabama Air National Guard, Montgomery ANGB/Dannelly Field
  100th Fighter Squadron 'Red Tails': F-16C/D

192nd Fighter Wing, Virginia Air National Guard, Langley AFB
  149th Fighter Squadron: F-22A ■

The Colorado Air National Guard flew F-16 Fighting Falcons to Amari Air Base in Estonia to participate for the first time in Sabre Strike 18 - a multinational and US multi-service exercise conducted at locations throughout the Baltic region and Poland. (Photo: US Air National Guard, Senior Master Sgt John Rohrer)

SUBSCRIBE
TO YOUR FAVOURITE MAGAZINE
AND SAVE

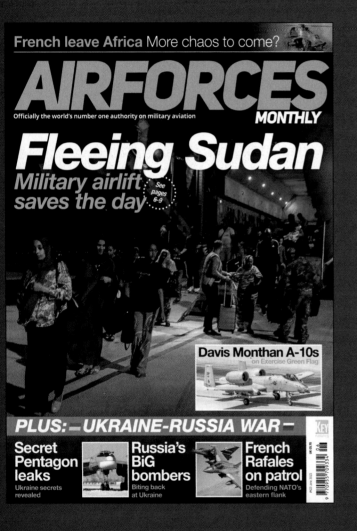

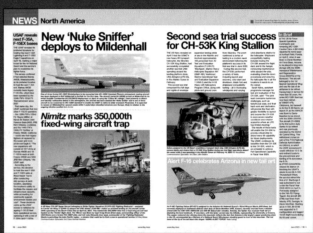

A US Air Force F-15C Eagle flies over the US Central Command area of responsibility in support of Operation Inherent Resolve, on July 7, 2020. The aircraft, from the 44th Fighter Squadron at Kadena, wears the name Night Train, and nose art depicting a skeletal, six-gun toting cowboy. The F-15C carries a centreline Sniper pod for long range passive target identification. (Photo: US Air Force, Staff Sgt Justin Parsons)

F-15C/D Eagle

The F-15C and its two-seat trainer version, the F-15D, are likely to be the first tactical fighter aircraft to disappear from the USAF's current 'seven type' frontline fleet.

The Eagle has already been retired from the last frontline active duty fighter squadron, and the four remaining ANG F-15C/D units will soon follow. The basic Eagle airframe design, will, however, be around for a while, in the shape of the derived F-15E Strike Eagle and the F-15EX Eagle II. And its twin-finned, twin-engined, high wing configuration will also live on, having influenced the Su-27 and MiG-29 families – and perhaps even some of the twin-finned fifth generation fighter designs.

The F-15 Eagle is an extremely agile, all-weather fighter that was designed and optimised to gain and maintain air supremacy over the battlefield. The F-15 Eagle was the world's dominant air-superiority fighter for more than 30 years and achieved an enviable record of 104 air-to-air kills in combat without loss. Even today, the F-15C can provide more modern fighters with a challenging opponent, though its reign is now drawing to a close.

Though it is unremarkable today, the F-15 was one of the first single-seat fighters with weapons and flight control systems that could be operated by a single pilot, safely and effectively. Before the Eagle, most heavy BVR fighters were two-seaters.

Though we take them for granted in 2023, the F-15 was unusual in having a true multi-mission avionics system with a head-up display, advanced radar, an internally mounted, tactical electronic-warfare system, inertial navigation system, UHF communications, a tactical navigation system and an instrument landing system.

With a wing area roughly equal to the size of a squash court (and not, as frequently and inaccurately claimed, the size of a tennis court), and a maximum take-off weight of 68,000 pounds, the F-15C has a low wing loading, while two afterburning Pratt & Whitney F100-PW-100 engines each produce 23,450lb of thrust (conferring a high thrust-to-weight ratio), giving the Eagle remarkable agility and performance for an aircraft of its size, and even allowing the aircraft to accelerate in a vertical climb when lightly loaded. The aircraft also had a roomy cockpit, in which the pilot sat high under a bubble canopy, giving him an unrivalled all-round view.

The Eagle's sheer performance allowed a lightly modified single-seat F-15A development aircraft to break eight time-to-climb world records between January 16 and February 1, 1975. On the last of these flights, the so-called 'Streak Eagle' reached an altitude of 98,425ft just three minutes and 27.8 seconds from brake release, and then 'coasted' on to nearly 103,000ft before descending.

But although the F-15 is a formidable dogfighter, the aircraft was always much more than that, and it was optimised from the start to win the beyond visual range (BVR) fight, picking off its enemies before they realised that the F-15 was even there. To achieve this, the Eagle used very long range missiles, backed up by a short range armament that included IR-homing missiles and a powerful internal gun. This was the tried and tested six-barrel 20mm M61A1 Vulcan cannon (with up to 940 rounds of ammunition) – selected after the failure of

F-15C Eagles from the 493rd Fighter Squadron travel back to RAF Lakenheath, United Kingdom after participating in exercise Baltic Trident at Ämari Air Base, Estonia, on March 19, 2021. Aircraft and airmen from the 48th Fighter Wing were in Estonia for an Agile Combat Employment exercise with NATO and partner forces in the Baltic Region. (Photo: US Air Force, Airman 1st Class Jessi Monte)

efforts to produce a new 25mm GAU-7 cannon for the aircraft.

The F-15's missile armament was initially not very different to that of the F-4E Phantom it replaced in USAF service – with semi-active radar homing AIM-7F (later AIM-7M) Sparrows and IR-homing AIM-9J (later AIM-9P) Sidewinders. The original intention had been to use the new AIM-82 AAM, which had a 50° off boresight capability, but this was soon abandoned.

The F-15 also has a large nose, allowing the aircraft to carry a powerful radar with a big diameter antenna array. The APG-63 radar originally fitted was the first of a new generation of modern pulse-Doppler radars which had a genuine look-down/shootdown capability.

The F-15 was also designed to have a very long range, using so-called FAST (fuel and sensor tactical) packs which carried an additional 750 US gal of fuel. These new ▶

F-15C Eagles assigned to the 48th Fighter Wing pop IR decoy flares during a flight in support of Bomber Task Force Europe 20-2 over the North Sea on March 16, 2020. The withdrawal of the F-15Cs from Lakenheath left a gap in dedicated air dominance capability within USAFE. (Photo: US Air Force, Master Sgt Matthew Plew)

The AIM-120 AMRAAM is the F-15C's primary weapon, offering a very long range capability against enemy aircraft. The AMRAAM is due to be replaced in USAF service by the AIM-260 JATM, but the F-15C will be gone by then! (Photo: US Air Force)

semi-conformal fuel tanks were intended to allow long range deployments without tanker support. An early test aircraft demonstrated this, deploying from Loring AFB, Maine, to RAF Bentwaters in Suffolk without inflight refuelling, prior to its appearance at the 1974 Farnborough Air Show.

All of this gave the aircraft tremendous potential in the air-to-air role.

The original F-15 Eagle had significant air-to-ground potential, though this was left largely latent, as the USAF wanted a dedicated air superiority fighter and famously ordered: "Not a pound for air to ground." Another possible role for the F-15 emerged in the early 1980s. The F-15's extraordinary performance prompted the USAF to undertake trials of the Vought ASM-135A Anti-Satellite (ASAT) missile in 1984 and 1985, launching several of these weapons from a zoom-climbing F-15. Unfortunately, the ASAT tests breached a US-USSR treaty that banned the use of weapons in space, and Congress cut funding for the programme. The USAF terminated the development of the anti-satellite mission in 1988. But it had shown what was possible!

The official USAF factsheet suggests that the F-15 "can penetrate enemy defenses and outperform and outfight any current enemy aircraft." This is something of an exaggeration and is a claim that would prompt some Indian Su-30MKI pilots to raise an eyebrow, while the latest Russian fighters – like the Su-35S – have capabilities that could make them a serious threat. The capabilities of Russian and Chinese 'fifth generation' aircraft remain largely unknown, but it would seem to be complacent to assume that the F-15C still enjoys much of an edge over enemy fighters.

But the F-15C/D does remain viable against most threats, and the most highly upgraded examples of the breed do have AESA radars powerful enough to give their pilots 'first look' against most Russian or Chinese fighters, allowing them to detect, acquire, track and attack enemy aircraft before they can themselves be engaged.

Eagle history

The studies that eventually led to the F-15 began in April 1965, when Air Force Systems Command FX studies recommended a 60,000lb VG design, with air-air and air-ground capability. An RFP for concept formulation for a TSA (Tactical Support Aircraft) was issued to 13 companies in December 1965, and eight bids were submitted in March 1966. McDonnell Douglas were unsuccessful but continued in-house studies on the company's Model 199 from April to December 1966 without funding. The USAF, unhappy with the successful bids, ran its own Concept Formulation Study from the Autumn of 1966, settling on a 40,000lb, manoeuvrable 'Blue Bird' concept, resulting in the issue of a new Fighter, Experimental (FX) concept in August 1967. This time, McDonnell-Douglas and General Dynamics were issued study contracts. McDonnell-Douglas recommended a fixed wing, twin-engined, single seat fighter, and stuck to this formula through subsequent concept and contract definition phases.

By this time, the air war in Vietnam was going badly, with a kill: loss ratio that was in danger of becoming unfavourable, and far short of the 7:1 that the USAF had achieved in Korea. The answer seemed to be to acquire a better air-to-air fighter, and one that was not handicapped by the compromises that were limiting the F-4 Phantom.

Proposals from Fairchild-Hiller, North American, and McDonnell-Douglas were evaluated, and the McDonnell-Douglas Model 199B was announced as the winner (McDonnell Douglas had been placed first in all phases of the competition and also had the lowest contract price) and was awarded the Advanced Tactical Fighter contract – to build a new fighter designated as the F-15 - on December 23, 1969.

James S. McDonnell, founder of McDonnell Aircraft, christened the F-15 as the Eagle on June 26, 1972 and a month later, on July 27, test pilot Irv Burrows took the first F-15 Eagle for its maiden flight at Edwards Air Force Base in California. Just six months later, the

An AIM-9 Sidewinder streaks off the rail of an F-15C. (Photo: US Air Force)

The pilot of a US Air Force F-15 Eagle fires an AIM-120 Advanced Medium Range Air-to-Air Missile at a QF-4 Rhino full-scale aerial target drone during a Combat Archer mission over the Gulf of Mexico on July 21, 2005. The Eagle was assigned to the 131st Fighter Wing, 110th Fighter Squadron, St. Louis Missouri Air National Guard, and was deployed to Tyndall to participate in the Air-to-Air Weapons System Evaluation Program. (Photo: US Air Force, Master Sgt Michael Ammons)

US Air Force approved the Eagle for full-rate production.

The first flight of the two-seat F-15B (formerly TF-15A) trainer was made in July 1973. F-15As and two-seat F-15B trainer variants were delivered between 1974 and 1979. The F-15A entered the USAF inventory in November 1974, attaining IOC in September 1975. The first Eagle destined for a combat squadron was delivered in January 1976, when the 1st Tactical Fighter Wing at Langley began conversion to the F-15A, and new wings soon stood up at Bitburg in Germany, and Holloman AFB in New Mexico.

The F-15C and its two-seat trainer version, the F-15D, began replacing the F-15A/B from 1979. These new variants incorporated a number of Production Eagle Package (PEP 2000) improvements, including an increased maximum take-off weight of up to 68,000lb, 2,000lb of additional internal fuel, and provision for carrying conformal external fuel tanks.

The F-15C/D has received a succession of upgrades and improvements since it entered service. The F-15 Multistage Improvement Program (MSIP) was initiated in February 1983, with the first production MSIP F-15C aircraft being produced in 1985. MSIP enhanced the F-15C's tactical capabilities adding an upgraded central computer; a Programmable Armament Control Set, and an expanded Tactical Electronic Warfare System with improvements to the ALR-56C radar warning receiver and the ALQ-135 countermeasure set.

F-15C and D models were deployed to the Persian Gulf in 1991 in support of Operation Desert Storm and accounted for 34 of the USAF's 37 air-to-air victories. Since then, F-15Cs have been deployed for air expeditionary force deployments and for operations Southern Watch (no-fly zone in southern Iraq), Provide Comfort in Turkey, Allied Force in Bosnia, Enduring Freedom in Afghanistan, and Iraqi Freedom in Iraq.

The AN/APG-63 radar lay at the heart of the Eagle's success. The basic radar received a major upgrade in 1979, becoming the first airborne radar to incorporate a software programmable signal processor (PSP), which allowed the incorporation of new modes and the integration of new weapons through software reprogramming rather than by hardware retrofit. The APG-63 with PSP was one of the most important features that distinguished the F-15C/D from the earlier F-15A/B.

A close up view showing an AIM-9X Sidewinder short-range, heat-seeking air intercept missile attached to the port side inboard wing pylon of a US Air Force F-15C Eagle aircraft assigned to Detachment 1, 28th Test Squadron, at Nellis Air Force Base, Nevada, during an evaluation flight conducted over the Gulf of Mexico. (Photo: US Air Force)

This F-15C wore a heritage scheme in honour of wartime B-17 bombardier, 2d Lt David Kingsley, who won a posthumous Medal of Honor after giving his own parachute to a wounded gunner. The aircraft was assigned to the 173rd Fighter Wing at Kingsley Field Air National Guard Base in Oregon. (Photo: US Air National Guard, Senior Master Sgt Jennifer Shirar)

The final 43 production F-15Cs were fitted with the F-15E's APG-70 radar, which was a redesign of the APG-63 optimised for easier maintenance and better reliability. To reduce production costs, many of the AN/APG-70 modules were taken from the F/A-18's AN/APG-73 radar, with 85% commonality with the processors used in the F-14's AN/APG-71 radar.

Other F-15C/Ds were retrofitted with the AN/APG-63(V)1 radar, which was designed to replace outmoded APG-63 radars, providing improved performance and a tenfold increase in reliability while also providing significant mode growth opportunities. The new radar was able to track 14 targets simultaneously while simultaneously engaging six. Some 180 APG-63(V)1 radar systems were delivered to the US Air Force by Raytheon from October 2000 through to June 2005, at a rate of two to three radars per month.

This F-15C Eagle of the 493rd Fighter Squadron was painted in heritage colours commemorating a P-47 Thunderbolt predecessor, with a red and white chequered noseband and D-Day stripes around the wings and rear fuselage. (Photo: US Air Force, Tech Sgt Matthew Plew)

The first unit to receive a production AN/APG-63(V)1 system was the 27th Fighter Squadron at Langley Air Force Base, which received its first (V)1 equipped aircraft in March 2001.

An even bigger step in capability had been achieved in 2000, with the delivery of what was claimed to be the world's first operational AESA fighter radar to the Elmendorf Wing. This was the AN/APG-63(V)2, which combined a new AESA antenna array with the 'back end' hardware of the AN/APG-63(V)1 while retaining controls and displays that were nearly identical to those of its predecessor. The AESA radar had an exceptionally agile beam, providing nearly instantaneous track updates and enhanced multi-target tracking capability. Crucially, this allowed pilots to more fully take advantage of the AIM-120 AMRAAM's capabilities, simultaneously guiding multiple missiles to several targets that could be widely spaced in azimuth, elevation, and range. The new AESA array also brought improved pilot situational awareness, a three-fold increase in reliability and a new cruise missile defence capability. The 18 AESA-equipped aircraft were used by the 12th and 19th Fighter Squadrons at Elmendorf Air Force Base, Anchorage Alaska. The APG-63(V)2-equipped F-15C aircraft were transferred to Kadena in 2008.

In 2004 the air force changed its plans to upgrade 400 F-15s with the APG-63(V)1, deciding instead to install the APG-63(V)3 AESA radar. By the end of its career, the F-15C fleet was entirely AESA-equipped, though most (and perhaps all) two-seat F-15Ds remained equipped with the mechanically-scanned AN/APG-63(V)0.

Armament improvements included the replacement of the AIM-7 Sparrow with the AIM-120 advanced medium range air-to-air missile (AMRAAM) and the adoption of new,

more effective versions of the short-range IR-homing AIM-9 Sidewinder, culminating in integration of the latest AIM-120D and AIM-9X variants.

Some further F-15C/D upgrades have been scaled back. Plans to integrate the Eagle Passive/Active Warning Survivability System (EPAWSS) were cancelled altogether, while fewer aircraft than had originally been planned gained higher capacity, jam-resistant Link 16, and UHF satcom systems.

In February 2022, Air Combat Command (ACC) announced that its latest sensor pod, the Lockheed Martin Legion infrared search and track (IRST) pod had reached initial operating capability (IOC) on the type. An F-15C Eagle successfully fired an AIM-120 using IRST guidance for the first-time during tests with the pod at Eglin on August 5, 2021. The Legion pod uses the infrared spectrum to provide a passive detection and tracking capability at extended ranges or to track enemy aircraft in radar-denied environments.

Though two-thirds of the F-15C/D fleet have exceeded their design lives and suffer performance-limiting structural issues, the USAF determined that a planned fleetwide SLEP (Service Life Extension Programme) was not cost-effective and limited mods to only 63 airframes through FY22.

But though the Eagle retains a compelling performance and a winning blend of capabilities, it lacks the Low Observable (stealth) characteristics that are increasingly becoming de rigeur in the key frontline types. That does not mean that the F-15C did not have a vital role to play in US fighter operations, and that role extends beyond the Homeland Defense Alert mission.

When the stealthy F-22 entered service, the USAF developed integrated combat tactics

which saw operations by mixed formations of four F-15Cs and a pair of F-22s. These tactics maximised the strengths of both types - providing more options and flexibility. Having 5th generation aircraft to accomplish initial operations in a highly contested engagement zone was obviously essential, but using F-15s to supplement them, bringing additional firepower, mass and sensor capabilities could make the difference between success and failure.

Upgrades to sensors and avionics have kept the USAF's F-15C/D fleet viable until now, but over the type's 50-year career, the aircraft has been 'ridden hard and put away wet' and most individual F-15C and F-15D airframes are now tired and worn out, and are close to the end of their lives, structurally speaking.

The remaining active duty F-15C fleet began to be withdrawn in April 2022, when the F-15Cs of the 493rd Fighter Squadron 'Grim Reapers' left their long-time home at RAF Lakenheath, ending 45 years of F-15 air superiority operations in Europe. The final operational sortie was flown by F-15C 86-0172 on April 21, 2022, and the last four 493rd FS F-15C Eagles flew to Barnes Municipal Airport, Massachusetts on April 27, 2022.

In the Far East, the withdrawal of F-15Cs from the last remaining active duty F-15C units, the 44th Fighter Squadron 'Vampire Bats' and the 67th Fighter Squadron 'Fighting Cocks' at Kadena AB, Japan, began on December 1, 2022. The 18th Wing hosted the Kadena Eagle Sunset Celebration, from April 14-15.

After the PACAF/USAFE withdrawals (53 from PACAF and 20 from USAFE/AFAFRICA), 159 F-15C/Ds were left in the US inventory, including 122 single-seaters and 14 two-seaters with the Air National Guard, 18 F-15Cs and three F-15Ds with ACC and two F-15Cs with AFMC. ▶

Members of the 144th Maintenance Squadron and the Aircraft Maintenance Squadron painted this California Air National Guard F-15C Eagle aircraft in gaudy stars and stripes colours to celebrate its reaching 10,000 flying hours. The aircraft was flown for the first time after receiving the paint scheme in October 2022. (Photo: US Air National Guard, Staff Sgt Mercedes Taylor)

Lt Col Jonathon Friedman of the 123rd Fighter Squadron, poses in front of an F-15C at Portland Air National Guard Base, on March 22nd, 2023 shortly after reaching 2,000 flying hours in the F-15C. He is likely to be one of the last Oregon guardsmen to do so, with the upcoming arrival of the F-15EX. (Photo: US Air National Guard, Tech Sgt Alexander Frank)

Sixty-seven F-15C/D are to be divested under the Fiscal Year 2023 proposed budget, and 57 more in FY 2024.

The remaining Eagles fly with the Florida Air National Guard at Jacksonville ANGB (the 125th Fighter Wing's 159th Fighter Squadron), the California Air National Guard at Fresno (the 144th Fighter Wing's 194th Fighter Squadron), the Louisiana Air National Guard at NAS/JRB New Orleans (the 159th Fighter Wing's 122nd Fighter Squadron), the Massachusetts Air National Guard at Barnes Air National Guard Base (the 104th Fighter Wing's 131st Fighter Squadron) and two squadrons of the Oregon Air National Guard. The 142nd Fighter Wing's 123rd Fighter Squadron operates from Portland while the 173rd Fighter Wing's 114th Fighter Squadron is based at Kingsley Field ANGB near Klamath Falls.

Air National Guard officials have said that they plan to assign F-35s or F-15EXs to every ANG unit that currently flies the F-15. The selection of bases for the F-35 and F-15EX is contingent on an environmental impact analysis, which will be completed by the spring of 2024 before a final selection, the air force said. Under the plans announced so far, Jacksonville and Barnes are scheduled to each receive 18 new fifth-generation F-35A Joint Strike Fighters.

The F-15C Eagle used as the 493rd Fighter Squadron flagship departs Royal Air Force Lakenheath, England, on April 27, 2022. The F-15Cs gave way to the fifth-generation fighter F-35A Lightning II. (Photo: US Air Force, Airman 1st Class Olivia Gibson)

The shape of things to come. An F-15C Eagle assigned to the 123rd Fighter Squadron, Portland Air National Guard Base, Oregon, taxis to the runway at Nellis Air Force Base, Nevada, on October 20, 2021, following an F-15EX Eagle II of the 85th Test and Evaluation Squadron. (Photo: US Air Force, William R. Lewis)

F-15EXs are planned for Naval Air Station Joint Reserve Base New Orleans, Louisiana, and for Fresno Air National Guard Base, California. The based 159th Fighter Wing and the 144th Fighter Wing are each expected to receive 18 F-15EXs.

The fates of the F-15C/D units at Kingsley Field and Portland Air National Guard Base, both in Oregon, remain undecided, but both units would seem likely to receive the F-15EX.

Even when the last USAF F-15C makes its final flight to the boneyard, single-seat, air superiority Eagles will continue to ply their trade elsewhere. Saudi Arabia still has four squadrons of F-15Cs, with a few F-15D trainers, while Israel still operates examples of the F-15A, F-15B, F-15C and F-15D (all locally known as the Baz) in two frontline squadrons. But it is Japan that is the major operator of the single-seat F-15,

with eight squadrons operating a total of 155 single-seat F-15Js and 44 two-seat F-15DJs, of 213 originally purchased.

About half of Japan's F-15s (68 F-15Js and 34 F-15DJs) underwent a Multi-Stage Improvement Program (MSIP) and will remain in service for many years (with an OSD currently set at 2045). The remaining 99 or so aircraft that did not go through MSIP are deemed to be unsuitable for further upgrades and will be replaced by the Lockheed-Martin F-35 Joint Strike Fighter.

On February 4, 2022, the Japan Ministry of Defense confirmed that 68 single-seat F-15Js will be upgraded through the Japan Super Interceptor (JSI) programme at a cost of 646.5bn Yen (US $5.62bn). The JSI upgrade (which will be undertaken in-country) will add a Raytheon

AN/APG-82(V)1 active electronically scanned array radar, BAE Systems' AN/ALQ-239 Digital Electronic Warfare System (DEWS), and new Advanced Display Core Processor II Mission System Computers and radios, as well as integration of new stand-off air-to-ground weapons including the Lockheed Martin AGM-158 JASSM (Joint Air-to-Surface Standoff Missile).

An October 2019 State Department approval for the Japanese F-15 upgrade, said that the programme could cover the upgrade of 'up to 98' aircraft, but the decision as to whether to upgrade 34 remaining post-MSIP two-seat F-15DJs, is still under discussion.

Had the USAF's F-15Cs had sufficient structural life remaining there is no reason that they could not have received a similar upgrade – an intriguing 'what might have been?'! ■

The F-15C is nearing the sunset of its long career. Most surviving aircraft will be replaced by the F-15EX. (Photo: US Air Force)

Fairchild Republic A-10C Thunderbolt II

The USAF finally has permission to divest its remaining A-10s – after years of Congressional resistance and public opposition.

Officially named the Thunderbolt II, but better known as the Warthog, the A-10C is a specialised CAS aircraft tasked with interdiction, Forward Air Controller-Airborne (FAC-A), CSAR, and Strike Control and Reconnaissance missions. The 281 aircraft fleet is almost exactly evenly divided between active duty and reserve component units.

The A-10C is loved and loathed in almost equal measure. Although the A-10 is a favourite of aviation enthusiasts, the aircraft's most famous capabilities are largely irrelevant today, and the USAF no longer wants or needs an aircraft answering the A-10A's description! Time and again the USAF has sought to retire the type and use the funding for more important and necessary capabilities, but Congress has repeatedly blocked USAF efforts to retire the A-10, preventing divestments, and repeatedly stopping the USAF from killing off the mighty Warthog! Even as recently as 2020, Congress denied the Air Force's request to retire A-10s in FY21 as well as a request to cut 42 aircraft from the fleet in FY22.

As a result, the future fighter roadmap involved '4+1' aircraft types – with the A-10 being the 'plus one'. But all that seems to be changing, and in March 2023, USAF Chief of Staff General Charles Q. Brown Jr. noted that the 4+1 fighter plan was "probably just 'four' now."

The general told the annual McAleese Defense Programs Conference in Washington, DC that: "We're retiring A-10s faster than we originally thought, and I think that's probably the right answer." He said that the A-10's close air support mission could be conducted by a variety of other platforms, albeit not in quite the same way. Significantly, Brown noted that combatant commands had not been asking for the A-10s, because it is a "single-mission airplane," while it was also felt that the low-and-slow-flying Warthog would not be able to survive in a fight against a peer nation threat with modern air defences.

Hitherto, there was a statutory mandate that required the service to finish F-35A initial operational test and evaluation (IOT&E) before A-10 divestments could proceed, but although this has not happened, and although the F-35A programme remains frozen in low-rate initial production, the US Air Force has asked lawmakers to waive the mandate so that A-10 divestments can proceed. A-10 divestments have been allowed in the final FY23 National Defense Authorization Act, though it is not known whether the statutory mandate has been waived or withdrawn.

"The A-10 is a great airplane … in an uncontested environment. The challenge is that we're going to be in more contested environments in the future," Brown pointed out.

The road to the A-10

A 1966 USAF study of existing close air support (CAS) capabilities showed that the Lockheed AH-56 Cheyenne helicopter selected

US Air Force Captains Andrew Glowa, lead, and William Piepenbring, both with the 74th Fighter Squadron out of Moody Air Force Base, Georgia, launch flares from two A-10C Thunderbolt II aircraft over southern Georgia, on August 18, 2014. (Photo: US Air Force, Staff Sgt Jamal D. Sutter/Released)

An A-10C Thunderbolt II aircraft operated by the 107th Fighter Squadron, Selfridge Air National Guard Base, Michigan firing its GAU-8 Avenger cannon. The A-10 is used primarily for close-air support missions. (Photo: US Air Force, Tech Sgt Daniel Heaton)

to meet the Army's Advanced Aerial Fire Support System (AAFSS) competition would be unable to meet all of the escort and fire suppression tasks that the DoD required. The USAF concluded that it should acquire a simple, effective, inexpensive, dedicated, and survivable CAS aircraft at least as capable as the A-1. The USAF therefore released a request for information to 21 defence contractors for the A-X (Attack Experimental) programme on March 6, 1967.

In May 1970, the USAF issued a more detailed and much-modified request for proposals for the AX aircraft - which would be the first USAF aircraft designed exclusively for CAS. The RFP specified a maximum speed of 460mph (400kts), a take-off distance of 4,000ft, an external load of 16,000lb and a 285 mile mission radius, while the unit cost was set at just US $1.4m (equivalent to about $10m today). The aircraft was to be able to loiter near battle areas for extended periods of time, and to operate under a 1,000ft cloud base with 1.5 mile visibility. It was at this point that the anti-tank role assumed a greater importance, and the decision was taken that the AX aircraft would be designed around a hard-hitting new 30-mm rotary cannon.

Six companies submitted proposals for the AX aircraft, and Northrop and Fairchild Republic were selected to build prototypes - which became the YA-9A and YA-10A, respectively. General Electric and Philco-Ford were selected to build and test competing prototypes of the seven-barrel GAU-8 Gatling gun to meet a separate requirement.

Two YA-10 prototypes were built in the Republic factory in Farmingdale, New York, and the first of these made its maiden flight on May 10, 1972 in the hands of pilot Howard 'Sam' Nelson. After trials and a fly-off against the competing Northrop YA-9 (a design that bore some resemblance to the Soviet Su-25), the USAF announced the YA-10's selection on January 18, 1973. General Electric was selected to build the GAU-8 cannon in June 1973. The YA-10 then had to undergo an additional fly-off in 1974 against the Ling-Temco-Vought A-7D Corsair II, the principal USAF attack aircraft at the time, to prove that a new attack aircraft was needed at all!

Production A-10s were built by Fairchild in Hagerstown, Maryland. The first production A-10 flew in October 1975, and deliveries to Davis-Monthan Air Force Base, Arizona, ▶

A US Air Force A-10 Thunderbolt II takes off from a Michigan State Highway in Alpena, Michigan, on August 5, 2021. Two A-10 Thunderbolt IIs from the 354th Fighter Squadron and two A-10s from the Michigan Air National Guard's 127th Wing landed on the state highway as part of exercise Northern Strike 21. This was the first time that the air force had purposely landed modern aircraft on a civilian roadway in the US. (Photo: US Air Force, Senior Airman Alex M. Miller)

Two A-10 Thunderbolt IIs release countermeasure flares over the US Central Command area of responsibility, on July 23, 2020. The left hand aircraft wears the markings of the AFRES 442nd Fighter Wing at Whiteman AFB, Missouri, while the other was assigned to the 190th Fighter Squadron, Idaho ANG. (Photo: US Air Force, Staff Sgt Justin Parsons)

commenced in March 1976, continuing until March 1984. The USAF declared IOC for the A-10A in October 1977.

Fairchild Republic's A-10 had large, straight wings, which were optimised for manoeuvrability at low airspeeds and very low altitude, and that also ensured that the

A-10 would be a stable and highly accurate weapons-delivery platform. The aircraft was optimised for operation from relatively short and austere runways to allow it to use forward airstrips close to the front lines, and the aircraft featured a sturdy landing gear, with low-pressure tyres. The aircraft was

also designed to be serviced and sustained from bases with limited facilities close to the battle area.

But the Cold War tank killer was built around the extraordinary 30mm GAU-8/A Gatling gun – famously described as being 'as big as a VW Beetle' and firing 3,900 rounds per minute – and the rounds were equally famously described as being 'the size of a milk bottle'. They were made using ultra-heavy, ultra-dense depleted uranium, to destroy an array of ground targets including tanks. And the A-10A carried 1,174 rounds of high-explosive incendiary (HEI) or HEI/armour-piercing incendiary ammunition for this monstrous cannon.

Complementing the A-10's agility, flexibility and lethality was an unparalleled degree of survivability. Many of the aircraft's parts are interchangeable left and right, including the engines, main landing gear and vertical stabilisers, facilitating battle damage repairs. Other systems were armoured or redundant, and the aircraft's self-sealing fuel tanks are protected by internal and external foam. The cockpit is protected by titanium armour which also protects parts of the flight-control system, resulting in an aircraft that was able to survive direct hits from armour-piercing and high explosive projectiles of up to 23-mm, absorbing battle damage and returning to base for repair. Manual systems back up the redundant hydraulic flight-control systems, allowing the pilot to continue to fly the aircraft even when hydraulic power is lost.

A US Air Force A-10 Thunderbolt II takes off from Davis-Monthan Air Force Base, Arizona, on June 1, 2022, laden with AGM-65 Maverick missiles. (Photo: US Air Force, Staff Sgt Jacob T. Stephens)

The A-10 has been the subject of regular upgrade programmes. In 1978, the Lockheed Martin AN/AAS-35(V) Pave Penny laser spot tracker was integrated, carried on a pylon mounted below the right hand side of the forward fuselage. The Pave Penny acts as a 'marked target seeker' detecting reflected laser energy from laser designators to allow the A-10 to deliver laser guided munitions. And, in 1980, the A-10 began receiving an inertial navigation system.

The A-10A proved its worth during the 1991 Gulf War (Operation Desert Storm), its anti-tank capability, long loiter and wide combat radius proving particularly useful. It demonstrated a 95.7% mission capable rate during the Gulf War, flying 8,100 sorties and launching 90% of the AGM-65 Maverick missiles used in the conflict.

In the early 1990s, the A-10 fleet began to undergo the Low-Altitude Safety and Targeting Enhancement (LASTE) upgrade. This introduced an Integrated Flight and Fire Control Computer (IFFCC) (a computerised weapon-aiming computer) providing a constantly computed impact point for the delivery of freefall ordnance, as well as an autopilot, and a ground-collision warning system.

Few of the A-10's unique capabilities were necessary in the post-Cold War environment, which saw close air support becoming a matter of delivering PGMs from medium altitude, where the A-10 offered little that other platforms did not, though it does enjoy

US airmen assigned to the 455th Expeditionary Maintenance Squadron (EAMXS), load 30mm ammunition onto an A-10 Thunderbolt II aircraft of the 188th Fighter Wing, the Flying Razorbacks, at Bagram Air Field, Parwan province, Afghanistan, on September 2, 2012. (US Army photo by 1st Lt Jared S. Blair/Released) (Photo: US Air Force)

a large combat radius, a long loiter time and the ability to carry up to 16,000lb of ordnance in addition to its (now little used) 30mm cannon. Using night-vision goggles, A-10C pilots can conduct their missions during darkness.

Enter the C

From 1999, A-10s began receiving Global Positioning System navigation systems and a new multi-function display. The fleet was further modernised under the Precision Engagement Program, which resulted in

➤

US Air Force Staff Sgt Journey Yanzick, 75th Expeditionary Fighter Generation Squadron weapons crew member, secures munitions onto a jammer before Senior Airman Christian Salas, 75th EFGS weapons crew member, lifts and transports it to be loaded onto US Air Force A-10 Thunderbolt II at Al Dhafra Air Base, United Arab Emirates on April 18, 2022. (Photo: US Air Force, Tech Sgt Alex Fox Echols III)

A US Air Force A-10 Thunderbolt II flies over Davis-Monthan Air Force Base, Arizona, on May 19, 2022. The aircraft is assigned to the A-10 Demonstration Team and wears a Vietnam heritage colour scheme to pay tribute to the 355th Tactical Fighter Wing's contributions in the Vietnam conflict. (Photo: US Air Force, Senior Airman Jacob T. Stephens)

a new variant, the A-10C. The A-10C added colour cockpit MFDs, a Helmet Mounted Cueing System (HMCS), hands on throttle and stick controls, a digital stores management system, and compatibility with GPS-guided weapons. The A-10C also introduced Litening/Sniper targeting pods, advanced data links, and integrated sensors.

The first A-10C first flew at Eglin on January 20, 2005, and the first upgraded aircraft were delivered from 2006 to 2012. The A-10C achieved IOC in September 2007 and made its combat debut during Operation Iraqi Freedom in 2007.

When Turkey authorised US flights from Incirlik during Operation Inherent Resolve, A-10Cs flew 1,600 sorties against 2,500 targets. The 12 A-10s of the 74th Expeditionary Fighter Squadron struck 44% of all so-called Islamic

State (ISIS) targets in Operation Inherent Resolve, winning the squadron the prestigious Gallant Unit Citation.

With night-vision goggles and targeting pods, the A-10C was able to operate under low cloud bases, even at night, while the 9,065lb thrust GE Aviation TF34-GE-100 turbofans were quiet and frugal, and the aircraft's ability to operate from unconventional runways has made the design potentially useful for the USAF's new strategy of agile combat employment. During exercise Northern Strike 21-2, Michigan Air National Guard A-10Cs practised operations from public highways.

A Wing Replacement Program is underway to enable 218 A-10Cs to remain operational until the 2030s. This programme builds on Boeing's so-called 'HOG UP' programme, which began in

1999, and which aimed to increase the aircraft's life to 16,000 flying hours. This programme also included replacing primary cockpit instruments with a high-resolution digital glass display, adding directional audio threat cueing, modernising ARC-210 UHF/ VHF comms, adding Ethernet, and integrating the Small Diameter Bomb I.

A fleetwide re-winging was organised under the Thick-skin Urgent Spares Kitting (TUSK) programme, with 218 aircraft originally slated for retrofit through to FY 2030. The base contract was for 117 wings with options for 125 additional wings. Of these, 173 wings are now on order with options remaining for 69 additional wings. In 2014, the USAF considered

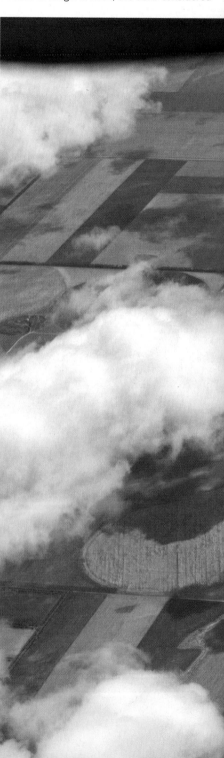

A black and grey US Air Force A-10 Thunderbolt II from the Indiana Air National Guard's 122nd Fighter Wing 'Blacksnakes,' flying home on July 7, 2021, after being painted at the Air National Guard paint facility in Sioux City, Iowa. The paint scheme, a departure from the standard two-tone grey, was created by request in order to commemorate the 100th anniversary of aviation in the Indiana National Guard. (Photo: US Air National Guard, Senior Master Sgt Vincent De Groot)

A-10 Thunderbolt IIs assigned to Whiteman Air Force Base, arrive at Kandahar Airfield, Afghanistan, on January 19, 2018. US Air Forces Central Command realigned airpower to USFOR-A Combined-Joint Area of Operations (CJOA) to support increased operations in support of the Resolute Support Mission and Operation Freedom's Sentinel. (Photo: US Air Force, Staff Sgt Sean Martin)

halting the wing replacement programme as part of its plans to retire the A-10. It was calculated that this could save $500m, though by May 2015 the re-winging programme was finally judged to be too advanced to be efficiently cancelled.

Two A-10s flew with the new wings fitted in November 2011, and this improved mission readiness, decreased maintenance costs, and promised to allow the A-10 to be operated up to 2035 if necessary.

There are 281 A-10s in the inventory of 713 aircraft built. Some 141 of these serve with Active Duty units, 85 with the Air National Guard and 55 with Air Force Reserve Command, with an average age of 40.3 years. ➤

A pilot of the 190th Fighter Squadron, 124th Fighter Wing, Boise, Idaho, flies an A-10 Thunderbolt II with a newly painted heritage paint scheme home from the Air National Guard's paint facility in Sioux City, Iowa to its new home at the Idaho Air National Guard, Gowen Field, Idaho, on May 12, 2021. The heritage A-10 aircraft was painted to commemorate the 190th FS's 75th Anniversary and made to mimic a 1944 P-47 Thunderbolt flown in WWII by the 405th Fighter Squadron, which was later re-designated as the 190th FS. (Photo: US Air National Guard, Staff Sgt Mercedee Wilds)

An A-10 Thunderbolt II assigned to the 422nd Test and Evaluation Squadron takes off for a test mission at Nellis Air Force Base, on April 19, 2023, armed with 16 GBU-39 small diameter bombs. (Photo: US Air Force, William R. Lewis)

Authorization Act, and 42 more A-10s are due to follow these into retirement in 2024. Air Combat Command is prioritising the A-10s with the least combat effectiveness for retirement first to ensure the most combat capable airframes remain in service.

The first A-10C unit to disappear will be the 122nd Fighter Wing ('Blacksnakes') at Fort Wayne, Indiana, which will re-equip with F-16s in 2023.

The first of the 21 aircraft to be retired this year, 80-0149 of the 74th Fighter Squadron at Moody AFB was flown to Davis Monthan on April 5, 2023, after 'clocking up' 14,125 flight hours, with Captain Kevin Domingue at the controls. The aircraft joined 100 A-10s (49 A-10As and 51 A-10Cs) already stored at the Desert Boneyard. The 74th is not running down its A-10 inventory, however, and the withdrawn aircraft has already been replaced by a replacement A-10C from Fort Wayne Air National Guard Base.

Air Force Chief of Staff General CQ Brown has said that: "The A-10 will probably be out of the USAF inventory over the next five or six years." He explained that combatant commands had been reluctant to request the aircraft due to its limited close air support role. "A-10s are not the things they're asking for. As a matter of fact, I'm having difficulty having them use A-10s because it's kind of a single-mission airplane."

Brown believes that other platforms in the US Air Force inventory can perform close air support, pointing out that precision guided munitions allow CAS to be undertaken in a different way to the traditional 'low and slow' tactics used by the A-10 in days gone by. Indeed, with an increasingly contested environment, this change is absolutely necessary.

These serve in the interdiction, Forward Air Controller-Airborne (FAC-A), CSAR, and Strike Control & Reconnaissance roles with two active duty squadrons and one AFRC unit of the 23rd Wing at Moody AFB, GA, the 53rd Wing at Eglin AFB, FL, the 57th Wing at Nellis AFB, NV, and with two more active duty squadrons belonging to the 355th Wing at Davis Monthan AFB, AZ within Air Combat Command, where two AFRC squadrons are assigned to the co-located 924th Fighter Group. A-10Cs also serve with PACAF's 51st FW at Osan AB, South Korea.

ANG units include the 122nd FW at Fort Wayne Airport, Indiana, the 124th FW at Gowen Field (Boise Air Terminal), Idaho, the 127th Wing at Selfridge ANGB, Michigan, the 175th Wing at Warfield ANGB, Martin State Airport, Maryland. AFRC controls the A-10s of the 442nd FW and the 495th Fighter Group at Whiteman AFB, Missouri, the 926th Wing at Nellis AFB, Nevada, and the 944th FW, a classic and active associate unit at Luke AFB, AZ.

Some 21 Thunderbolts have been authorised to be retired under the FY23 National Defense

US Air Force Captain Coleen Berryhill, 74th Fighter Squadron A-10C Thunderbolt II pilot, flies above a formation of B1-B Lancer and A-10 aircraft over the Philippine Sea, on November 9, 2022. These aircraft were brought to the Indo-Pacific region in conjunction with Operation Iron Thunder, a Dynamic Force Employment operation exercising PACAF's ability to remain strategically predictable, but operationally unpredictable in an ever-evolving competitive and contested environment. (Photo: US Air Force, Capt Coleen Berryhill)

An A-10 Thunderbolt II loaded with a DATM-160 Miniature Air-Launched Decoy (MALD) on the runway at San Clemente Island, California, on November 7, 2022 during a Green Flag-West training exercise. (Photo: US Air Force, Airman 1st Class Trevor Bell)

The A-10C community has been quick to demonstrate that the aircraft is not a 'one trick pony', and that the Warthog can contribute to future high-end combat operations, perhaps especially in any potential conflict against China in the Pacific. During Operation Iron Thunder in November 2022, A-10Cs from the 74th Fighter Squadron at Moody Air Force Base flew a simulated integrated strike mission with B-1B Lancers over the Philippine Sea, employing ADM-160 Miniature Air Launched Decoys (MALD) to support the bombers by neutralising the enemy's air defence system and cluttering radar detection systems through the use of decoys from stand-off range. The 74th FS demonstrated that the A-10C was well suited to launching large groups of these MALDs to help protect other aircraft, increasing the probability that those aircraft and weapons could successfully strike their targets.

"Once the A-10s have completed a MALD employment mission, those A-10s have the ability to maximize their long loiter times to be available for additional taskings such as air operations in support of maritime surface warfare," said Lieutenant Colonel Matt Shelly, commander of the 74th Fighter Squadron.

"The A-10 also brings unique flexibility to the combatant commander with its ability to operate in austere locations with minimal support requirements.

"To remain combat effective for the next conflict, the A-10 community must accelerate change or lose. The A-10 is famous for its 30-millimeter Gatling gun and its ability to carry large weapons loads, but we must move beyond the weapons and mission sets that made the A-10 famous in the low-intensity conflicts of the Middle East and accelerate change in this way to be a force multiplier for combatant commanders."

Captain Coleen Berryhill, a pilot with the 74th Fighter Squadron A-10C said: "This mission was a fantastic way to demonstrate how the A-10 is capable of shifting from a close air support team mindset to a strike team. We are building on our old principles to transform into the A-10 community the joint force needs."

Even as its retirement draws closer, the A-10 is increasingly demonstrating its usefulness. As the air force's broader focus has shifted to the Pacific (and latterly to Europe), it has become more difficult to make forces available to

CENTCOM, and to meet its requirement for two and a half fighter squadrons.

General Michael 'Erik' Kurilla, the head of US Central Command (CENTCOM), told the House Armed Services Committee that: "I have a requirement for additional air assets," and confirmed that A-10s had been approved to deploy to CENTCOM from April 2023, making up part of a deployed force of manned aircraft, augmenting F-15E Strike Eagles and F-16C Fighting Falcons.

The first A-10 Thunderbolt II aircraft arrived in the US Central Command area of responsibility on March 31, 2023, joining the 380th Air Expeditionary Wing at Al Dhafra Air Base, United Arab Emirates, where they formed the 75th Expeditionary Fighter Squadron and 75th Expeditionary Fighter Generation Squadron. The A-10Cs deployed were drawn from Moody Air Force Base, Georgia, and flew their first live-fire sorties on April 18, 2023.

There remains concern that withdrawal of the A-10C will lead to an erosion of US CAS capabilities and competences.

As long ago as 2016, Michael Gilmore, then the Pentagon's director of operational test and evaluation, confirmed that the F-35 was intended to succeed the A-10. He said that the F-35 would rely on the F-22 for winning air superiority while assuming the F-16 role as the low end of the USAF high-low fighter mix strategy and replacing the A-10. It was made absolutely clear that the F-35 would take a very different approach to the close-air-support role.

The air force has described close air support as a secondary mission for F-35 pilots across its active duty, National Guard, and reserve components, which means that those pilots have to be familiar but not proficient in the role.

Some believe that there has been very little CAS training for F-35 pilots and that they are not required to fly any actual or simulated CAS training missions, compared to A-10 pilots who were required to fly between 13 and 20 CAS training missions, and who usually flew 32 additional CAS sorties. The Project on Government Oversight (POGO) has said that the only F-35 air force pilots required to fly close-air-support missions are those attending the USAF Weapons Course – and that just two of the 21 sorties that Weapons Course students fly are devoted to CAS! ∎

A 74th Fighter Generation Squadron load crew equips an A-10C Thunderbolt II with a Miniature Air-Launched Decoy craft at Andersen Air Force Base, Guam, November 4, 2022. The MALD is designed to negate enemy air defense systems and thereby allow previously vulnerable aircraft to operate in heavily contested environments. (Photo: US Air Force, Staff Sgt Hannah Malone)

Two F-22s of the 302nd Fighter Squadron fly at low level over the Alaskan snow. The nearest aircraft has extended its AIM-9 Sidewinder launch trapeze, since weapons are usually carried internally to preserve the aircraft's low radar cross section. (Photo: US Air Force)

Lockheed Martin F-22 Raptor

Though it is widely acknowledged as being the most capable air dominance fighter in the world, the F-22 is set for retirement and fated to be outlived by the F-15E and F-16!

The Lockheed Martin F-22 Raptor is perhaps the most surprising 'casualty' of the USAF's planned reduction to four fighter fleets. Surprising because the F-22 is still the world's most capable fighter, providing unprecedented air dominance. Before the Raptor, people used the tag 'air superiority' – defined as being the ability for friendly operations to proceed at a given time and place without prohibitive interference from opposing forces. Air superiority provides freedom of action, freedom from attack, freedom to attack, and freedom of access. Air supremacy goes further, whereby the enemy air force is incapable of effective interference anywhere within a given theatre of operations. Air dominance can be defined as complete control of the air, with the ability to dictate the terms and conditions of any engagement.

The F-22 forms a critical component of the USA's Global Strike Task Force, and is designed to project air dominance, rapidly and at great distances and then to defeat any threats that might attempt to deny access to

US and allied force elements. And the Raptor is equally impressive in defensive or offensive operations – able to defend a particular point better than anything else, but with an unmatched ability to strike hard and deep and with great precision, and all while providing unmatched situational awareness to the rest of the force.

The fifth generation F-22 has a unique and devastating combination of agility, supercruise performance, low observability, and situational awareness, combined with an arsenal of lethal long-range air-to-air and air-to-ground weaponry. All of this makes it capable of penetrating and operating within even the most heavily contested airspace.

The Raptor's powerful sensors (including the class-leading AN/APG-77 AESA radar), integrated avionics and data links, permit simultaneous multitarget engagement, and make the Raptor the best air dominance fighter in the world, and make it what its manufacturer, Lockheed Martin, calls a pathfinder to the next generation of air dominance.

The F-22A's superiority over all other fighter aircraft is tacitly acknowledged even by rival manufacturers. Such rivals no longer claim to offer 'the best', but instead compete to claim that their fighters are second only to the Raptor! This makes the F-22 the yardstick against which other fighters are measured.

But 'best' is not necessarily the same as 'most useful', and the F-22 has not been used (or needed) in recent campaigns in Iraq or Afghanistan. The Raptor has had few opportunities to demonstrate its unique capabilities, and some believe that had the type been deployed in its current form it could easily have been more trouble than it would have been worth – lacking key capabilities for those campaigns, and hard to integrate with other assets.

But against an opponent with a modern integrated air defence infrastructure, things would be very different. Only the 'fifth generation' capabilities of the F-22 would give the USA the ability to operate with impunity in a battlespace defended by 'double digit' SAMs, and only the F-22 could provide politically sustainable exchange ratios against 'high end' enemy fighters (developed derivatives of the Su-27 'Flanker', for instance).

Lockheed Martin coined the term 'fifth generation fighter' to describe the F-22A, originally defining this as encompassing 'designed in' advanced 'stealth' (low observability, especially to radar), extreme performance, sensor/information fusion and advanced sustainment. Before it needed to apply the 'fifth generation' tag to its F-35 Joint Strike Fighter, Lockheed Martin specifically included supercruise performance (the ability to achieve and maintain speeds in excess of Mach 1.5 for extended periods of time without the use of afterburners) and extreme agility as being key 'fifth generation' defining features too.

Uniquely among the world's in-service fighters, the F-22 has all of these features, making it the world's only true 'fifth generation' fighter and representing a quantum leap in lethality and survivability.

Programme History

In 1981 the US Air Force identified a requirement for an Advanced Tactical Fighter (ATF) to replace the F-15 Eagle and F-16 Fighting Falcon. The 'Senior Sky' programme aimed to achieve an ambitious leap in performance

An AIM-9 missile waits to be loaded as 325th Fighter Wing F-22A Raptors taxi out for a mission at Eglin Air Force Base, Florida. One squadron of Raptors and Talons moved to Eglin after Hurricane Michael devastated Tyndall Air Force Base in 2018. (Photo: US Air Force, Samuel King Jr.)

by taking advantage of new technologies, including stealth technology, new generation sensors and avionics, more powerful engines that would allow supersonic cruise in dry power, advanced flight control systems, and advanced composite materials and lightweight alloys. A request for information (RFI) was issued to the aerospace industry in May 1981. Two teams were selected to undertake a 50-month Dem/Val (Demonstration and Validation) phase, culminating in flight testing of two technology demonstrator aircraft. Lockheed, teamed with Boeing and General Dynamics offered the YF-23, while Northrop, teamed with McDonnell Douglas, offered the YF-23. Pratt & Whitney and General Electric were contracted to develop competing propulsion systems for the ATF.

>

US Air Force Captain Matthew Gibson, a pilot assigned to the 525th Fighter Squadron at Joint Base Elmendorf-Richardson, Alaska, climbs into the cockpit of a US Air Force F-22A Raptor at Kadena Air Base, Japan, on December 16, 2022. The deployment of newer and more advanced aircraft at Kadena AB strengthens the US posture in the region and compensates for the withdrawal of F-15Cs from Kadena. (Photo: US Air Force, Airman 1st Class Sebastian Romawac)

An F-22 Raptor assigned to the 192nd Fighter Wing, Virginia Air National Guard, Virginia flies over the Georgia coast during an air combat exercise at Sentry Savannah on May 5, 2022. Sentry Savannah is a joint force integrated exercise of fourth- and fifth-generation fighter jets, designed to showcase the air force's air combat readiness in preparation for tomorrow's fight. (Photo: US Air Force, Senior Airman Erica Webster)

The first of two prototype YF-22s made its maiden flight on September 29, 1990, and the Lockheed design was subsequently selected as the winner of the Advanced Tactical Fighter competition, to meet what was expected to be a requirement for 750 aircraft.

The aircraft underwent a minor redesign for production, with reduced leading edge sweep, smaller vertical stabilisers shifted further aft, and with changes to the canopy and intakes. The engineering and manufacturing development (EMD) effort began in 1991 and the first of eight production representative EMD F-22s (91-4001) made its maiden flight on September 7, 1997.

The aircraft entered low rate initial production in 2001, and The first production F-22A was delivered to Nellis AFB, Nevada, for Initial Operational Test and Evaluation (IOT&E) in January 2003. After the completion of the IOT&E phase, approval was given for full rate production in 2005. Deliveries of operational aircraft for pilot training at Tyndall AFB, Florida had started in September 2003, and the first combat ready F-22 was delivered to the 1st Fighter Wing at Langley AFB, Virginia, in January 2005. The aircraft was briefly known as the F/A-22 before it was re-designated as the F-22A in December 2005, at the same time that initial operating capability was declared. With no two-seat trainer built, the A-suffix has slipped into disuse in the years since then.

The Raptor flew its first operational sortie during Operation Noble Eagle in 2006 and made its debut in the air-to-ground role during Operation Inherent Resolve on September 22, 2014, dropping 1,000lb GPS-guided bombs on so-called Islamic State (ISIS) targets near Tishrin Dam.

The F-22 serves with the 1st Fighter Wing (ACC) at JB Langley-Eustis, VA; the 3rd Wing (PACAF) at JB Elmendorf-Richardson, Alaska; the 15th Wing (PACAF) at JB Pearl Harbor-Hickam, Hawaii; the 53rd Wing (ACC) at Eglin AFB, FL; the 57th Wing (ACC) at Nellis AFB, NV; and the 926th Wing (an AFRC classic associate unit) at Edwards AFB, CA.

Today the F-22 serves with two squadrons of Air Combat Command's 1st Fighter Wing at Langley Air Force Base, Virginia (plus an Air National Guard associate unit). Tyndall housed a training unit and an Air Force Reserve Command associate unit, but the training squadron relocated to Eglin after Hurricane Michael. Small numbers of aircraft fly with three test units at Nellis Air Force Base, Nevada, and Edwards Air Force Base, California.

An F-22 Raptor assigned to the 325th Fighter Wing, Tyndall Air Force Base, Florida takes off from the Air Dominance Center for an air combat exercise at Sentry Savannah on May 10, 2022. Sentry Savannah is the Air National Guard's largest air-to-air, joint aerial combat exercise for fourth- and fifth-generation fighters. The three dimensional thrust vectoring nozzles are apparent. (Photo: US Air Force, Senior Airman Erica Webster)

An F-22 Raptor assigned to the 525th Fighter Squadron takes off at Joint Base Elmendorf-Richardson, Alaska, on February 27, 2023, showing off its broad flat belly and large internal weapons bays. The F-22 forms a critical component of the Global Strike Task Force, and is designed to project air dominance, rapidly and at great distances to defeat threats. (Photo: US Air Force, Senior Airman Patrick Sullivan)

With PACAF, the type equips two squadrons of the 3rd Wing at Joint Base Elmendorf–Richardson, Alaska (plus an Air Force Reserve Command associate unit), and one squadron at JB Pearl Harbor-Hickam (the former Hickam Air Force Base), Hawaii (plus an Air National Guard unit).

The biggest problem with the F-22 is that there simply aren't enough of them, and the relatively tiny fleet of F-22s is undoubtedly costly and increasingly difficult to support, with a host of obsolescence/DMS issues, and some unique maintenance challenges.

The USAF had originally planned to buy a total of 750 ATF fighters, but high unit costs saw the programme cut back – increasing those unit costs, and resulting in further cutbacks, again and again. The programme was cut back to 648 aircraft, then 339, and then, in 2003, to 277 aircraft. The following year, the Department of Defense (DoD) further reduced the total to 183 operational aircraft, though the USAF's stated requirement was then for 381! Efforts were made to increase the total to 243, without success. The total was nudged up to 187 in 2008. Only 195 F-22s were built (eight test and 187 operational aircraft). With $28bn spent on research, development, and testing, and $34bn more on procurement, the average unit cost reached $339m per aircraft, though the incremental unit cost of one additional F-22 was calculated to be around $138m when proposals were made to restart production.

Lockheed built 74 Block 10/20 F-22 aircraft for training and 112 combat-coded Block 30/35 aircraft, with one further Block 30 aircraft dedicated to flight sciences at Edwards Air Force Base. Some 37 Block 20 aircraft from Lot 3 onward were subsequently upgraded to Block 30 standards, increasing the Block 30/35 fleet to 149 aircraft (125 of which are combat coded). Some 37 aircraft remain in the Block 20 configuration.

The Raptor described

The F-22 is able to outmanoeuvre and out-accelerate any threat, thanks to its sophisticated aerodynamic design, advanced flight controls, large control surfaces, thrust vectoring nozzles and high thrust-to-weight ratio. Unlike the Russian fighters that pioneered super-manoeuvrability and thrust-vectoring, the F-22's agility is not just for airshows, or last ditch defensive manoeuvres, and the aircraft has the ability to regain energy very rapidly.

The F-22's engines produce more thrust than any current fighter engine, allowing the sleek, low drag F-22 to accelerate rapidly, and to cruise at supersonic airspeeds without recourse to afterburner -- a characteristic known as ▶

A US Air Force F-22 Raptor assigned to the 90th Expeditionary Fighter Squadron flies with two Polish F-16s during the NATO Air Shielding media day, on October 12, 2022, at Łask Air Base, Poland. The event showcased the importance of NATO's Air Shielding mission and the interoperability among the US and NATO members.
(Photo: US Air Force, Staff Sgt Danielle Sukhlall)

supercruise. Supercruise enhances survivability and lethality by minimising exposure to enemy defences, engaging distant, time-critical targets without incurring range penalties.

The F-22's use of low-observable technologies provides significantly improved survivability and lethality against both air-to-air and surface-to-air threats and were said to have brought stealth into the day, unlike the F-117A which relied on stealth and darkness to remain undetected. Low observability delays enemy detection, and this, in conjunction with the ability to supercruise, can provide effective immunity from interception in some circumstances. Coupled with the Raptor's APG-77 AESA radar, stealth also guarantees that the F-22 will get the 'first look' against any adversary.

The F-22 has an advanced integrated avionics suite, with an array of sophisticated onboard sensors, and net-enabled, off-board sensors which present the pilot with a seamless real-time, intuitive, 360° view of the battlespace. This provides the Raptor pilot with unmatched situational awareness, and allows him to detect, locate, identify, track, and engage air-to-air threats before being detected himself. This enables him to enter the fight on his own terms.

The Northrop Grumman AN/APG-77 radar is probably the most advanced AESA radar in service today, with excellent performance and a 'low probability of intercept'. Radar emissions are automatically managed, so that signal intensity, duration and frequency are optimised to maximise pilot situational awareness while minimising any chance of those emissions being intercepted. The radar also incorporates an ultra-high resolution target recognition mode, offering centimetric resolution at extreme range. Returns are then matched to an onboard library to facilitate non-co-operative target recognition (NCTR).

Tom Burbage, former Lockheed F-22 programme manager once claimed that the Sanders AN/ALR-94 passive receiver system was "the most technically complex piece of equipment on the aircraft" describing it as "the most effective passive system ever installed on a fighter." ALR-94 can detect, track, and identify an enemy fighter radar at ranges of 250nm or more, determining the target's bearing, range, and type of any threat, and calculating the distance at which that threat radar will detect the F-22A. As the range closes, the ALR-94 can then cue the APG-77 to acquire the target and search for other aircraft in the hostile flight,

using minimum emissions to provide the precise range and velocity data needed to set up a BVR missile engagement. The ALR-94 can use a narrowband interleaved search and track (NBILST) mode to track an enemy fighter, and in some circumstances, can provide almost all of the information necessary to launch an AIM-120 AMRAAM.

The data from the AN/APG-77 radar, the AN/ALR-94 and offboard sensors can be correlated into a single track file, with more weight given to the most accurate sensor, such that the most accurate range may be provided by the APG-77, while the passive system may provide the most accurate azimuth data.

Ordnance

The F-22's bleeding edge sensors are augmented by powerful weapons.

To maintain low observability and reduce drag, the F-22 generally carries its weapons internally, in three weapons bays. The main weapons bay is on the bottom of the fuselage and accommodates LAU-142/A launchers for up to six AIM-120D AMRAAM beyond-visual-range missiles, though integration of the new AIM-260 JATM is already being planned. There are two smaller bays on the fuselage sides, aft of the engine intakes. These each accommodate an LAU-141/A launcher for single short-range AIM-9X missiles. The bay doors open for less than a second to launch a missile, using pneumatic or hydraulic rams to push missiles clear of the aircraft.

The Raptor can undertake both air-to-air and air-to-ground missions. Four of the missile launchers in the main weapons bay can be replaced by two bomb racks. These can each carry one 1,000lb bomb (such as a GBU-32 Joint Direct Attack Munition) or four 250lb small diameter bombs. The Raptor will still carry two AIM-120s and two AIM-9s in the air-to-ground configuration.

The Raptor's ability to drop weapons at very high speed can impart significant extra energy to any ordnance dropped, and it has been calculated that a JDAM dropped by a supercruising F-22 could have double the effective range compared to munitions dropped by legacy fast jet platforms. During tests, a 1,000lb JDAM dropped by an F-22 cruising at Mach 1.5 at 50,000ft hit a moving target at 24 miles range.

Though the F-22A demonstrated its ability to drop JDAM in June 2006, getting an operational air-to-ground capability took several years. Increment 3.1 software, tested in June 2009, provided a basic ground attack capability using Synthetic Aperture Radar mapping, and allowed limited use of the GBU-39 Small Diameter Bomb. Increment 3.2, fielded on the last 83 combat-coded Block 35s (and three test aircraft) finally gave an advanced SDB capability.

A US Air Force F-22 Raptor assigned to the 90th Fighter Squadron, 3rd Wing landing at the 32nd Tactical Air Base in Łask, Poland on August 4, 2022, laden with ferry tanks. The aircraft deployed to Poland to support the NATO Air Shielding in the European Theatre mission. (Photo: via US Air Force)

The first 34 Block 20 aircraft, used for test and training, did not have an air-to-ground capability at all.

Carrying two JDAMs or eight SDBs was felt to be a modest capability, and it was the lack of what Defense Secretary Robert Gates called "sufficient multi-mission capability for current military operations" that resulted in the Obama administration's decision to end F-22 production at just 187 fighters. This was a short-sighted decision, however, since the F-22's unique combination of advanced stealth, supercruise, manoeuvrability and integrated avionics allowed it to contribute ▶

Lt Col James Hecker flies over Fort Monroe before delivering the first operational F/A-22 Raptor to its permanent home at Langley Air Force Base, Virginia. This was the first of 26 Raptors to be delivered to the 27th Fighter Squadron. Colonel Hecker was the squadron's first commander. (Photo: US Air Force, Tech Sgt Ben Bloker)

The F-22's combination of sensors, stealth and supercruise underpin the aircraft's dominance in the air-to-air role. Here an F-22 fires an AIM-120 AMRAAM at a beyond visual range (BVR) target. (Photo: US Air Force)

to 'Day One', 'Kick down the door' operations, helping to facilitate freedom of movement for follow-on forces. It was precisely this capability that allowed the USAF to retire the F-117A (which never carried more than a pair of PGMs) from the inventory.

The synergy of agility, supercruise, stealth, integrated avionics and powerful weapons ensure F-22A lethality against all advanced air threats and also dramatically shrink enemy surface-to-air missile engagement envelopes thereby minimising opportunities for the enemy to track and engage the F-22.

Because of its ability to generate and share battlefield situational awareness the F-22 is a key enabler, helping friendly forces to operate safely and effectively even in the face of the most sophisticated enemy threat environment, guaranteeing air dominance (and not just air superiority).

Brickbats

But the F-22 does also have its downsides.

The F-22 has not overcome its early reputation as being something of a 'maintenance hog' and has consistently failed to meet the USAF's requirement for 12 hours of maintenance per flying hour. In 2009, it was revealed that the F-22 was requiring 34 maintenance man hours of per flying hour (MMH/FH) according to the Office of the Secretary of Defense or "just over 20 MMH/FH" according to

The F-22 does have a powerful air-to-ground capability – stealth and supercruise affording a degree of invulnerability from interception. This is the first guided JDAM launch, undertaken by Major John Teichert on 2 September, 2004. (Photo: US Air Force, Kevin Robertson)

Staff Sgt Michael Avalos, 325th Aircraft Maintenance Squadron, performs a walkaround check during the unit's quarterly weapons load competition at Eglin Air Force Base, Florida, with an AIM-9 Sidewinder on its extended launch trapeze. (Photo: US Air Force, Samuel King Jr.)

Lockheed. Things have got better since 2009, but not by much. There were reports of poor interchangeability of components between individual aircraft, corroding ejection seat rods (this caused a fleet-wide grounding in 2010). More fundamental design problems afflicted early aircraft, with leaky upper fuselage access panels on some aircraft, inadequate strength in the rear fuselage of the first 41 aircraft, and wing root attachment issues on the first 60 jets, while the first 91 aircraft built suffered fatigue problems with the forward fuselage bulkhead. All of these problems were eventually addressed through modifications and an enhanced inspection regime, but not without significant cost, and the aircraft's stealth coatings and canopy remain a particular maintenance burden. As a result, the F-22 has a 50% mission availability rate, far and away the worst in the USAF's tactical aircraft fleet, exacerbating the shortage of airframes.

In its Fiscal Year 2023 budget request, the air force proposed the withdrawal of 33 of its 36 remaining Block 20 F-22s, representing roughly 20% of the fleet, and currently forming the backbone of the training element at Eglin AFB. These aircraft are not felt to be operationally viable, with no air-to-ground capability, and one senior officer said that they were "not competitive" with China's latest J-20 stealth fighters.

The USAF also insists that these aircraft are no longer representative of the operational Block 35 they train pilots to fly. Lieutenant General Richard G. Moore Jnr, vice chief of staff for plans and programs, told the House Armed Services Committee's tactical aviation panel on March 29, that the Block 20 aircraft have so little commonality with the later Block 35 that pilots have to "unlearn" procedures used flying the Block 20 before they can become fully proficient in the Block 35.

The air force say that it would be cost prohibitive to upgrade the Block 20 aircraft, and that retiring them would save approximately US $2.5bn over five years – money that will instead be used for NGAD development. It has been estimated that it would cost $1.8bn to upgrade them (equivalent to $54.5m per aircraft, spread over eight years) with modern communications systems, electronic warfare capabilities and weapons and that any upgrade would take more than a decade to get started. This would be an unwelcome diversion and distraction from Lockheed Martin's F-35 Block 4 upgrade.

But the remaining F-22s are being kept viable through an 'agile' modernisation strategy that ensures a rapid and continuous process of developing, testing, and fielding incremental improvements to the aircraft. The fleet recently received Increment 3.2B software which added high-resolution SAR ground mapping, threat geolocation, EA capability, and integration of the SDB I, AIM-120D, and AIM-9X.

Ongoing upgrade efforts include the Reliability, Availability, and Maintainability Program (RAMP), which will improve electrical power generation, replace fibre optic avionics cables, and add more durable LO coatings (based on those of the newer F-35), as well as embodying structural and wiring fixes. This is in addition to the $350m structures retrofit programme that addressed improper titanium heat treatment in some airframe batches. All aircraft have now gone through a structural repair programme that adds another 8,000 flight hours to their usable airframe lives.

For many years, the F-22A did not have adequate means of contributing its full sensor picture to the rest of the force – a real shortcoming in an age of 'net centric warfare'. The aircraft has an excellent intra-flight data link that allows F-22As to share data almost ▶

Two US Air Force F-22 Raptor aircraft assigned to the 90th Fighter Squadron, Joint Base Elmendorf-Richardson, Alaska, fly alongside a US Air Force KC-135 Stratotanker aircraft over Poland on August 10, 2022. The F-22 is the most potent symbol of US air power and is regularly deployed wherever US interests are threatened. (Photo: US Air Force, Staff Sgt Kevin Long)

seamlessly, and work is underway to allow the aircraft to transfer more data off-board to legacy fourth generation aircraft such as the F-15 or F-16 (and to Command and Control platforms). Link 16 (previously TACLink-16) promises to enable two-way networking with legacy aircraft using Multifunctional Information Distribution System/Joint Tactical Radio System (MIDS/JTRS). Initial installs began in FY22, and fleet-wide upgrade is now planned for FY25.

Air force budget documents indicate that the USAF plans to spend more than $9bn upgrading its remaining F-22s through to the end of the decade, and upgrade priorities include improving tactical information transmission, combat identification, stealthy external fuel tanks, and electronic protection, but especially sensor systems improvements. The overall aim is to maintain air dominance and to preserve the Raptor's first look, first shot, and first kill capability against peer threats.

The Raptor Agile Capability Release (RACR) aims to provide a more agile route by which to integrate upgrades, instituting an annual cycle of software releases and minor internal hardware changes using rapid prototyping and rapid fielding acquisition processes. The first phase of RACR, known as Release 1 (R1), will function as the major hardware and software enabler for subsequent enhancements.

R1 provided an open-system architecture and finally saw the addition of a MIDS-JTRS terminal that enables the Raptor to fully use the standard Link 16 datalink protocol, including transmitting the Raptor's datalink 'picture'. R1 also includes Mode 5 IFF [identification friend-or-foe], which represents a significant step forward for the Raptor in terms of combat identification.

R1 developmental testing was completed on August 16, 2021, after 263 sorties, while Phase 1 Force Development Evaluation (FDE) added 286 sorties, and was followed by a shorter Phase 2 FDE. Operational squadrons started receiving the R1 upgrades in late 2022. R2 testing is now underway, and this will prepare the Raptor for the new AIM-260 Joint Air Tactical Missile (JATM). R3 will provide some upgrades to existing

The F-22 Demonstration Team aircraft at Patrick Space Force Base, Florida, on May 19, 2022. The F-22 configuration has come to be typical of stealth fighters, with canted vertical tails and edge alignment. (Photo: US Space Force, Senior Airman Thomas Sjoberg)

sensors and will expand the Link 16 capability to allow message sharing between allied forces.

A next generation air-to-air targeting sensor (a podded IRST sensor) for the F-22 has begun flight demonstration (perhaps under R2). Pictures of a test aircraft with two underwing pods are understood to show the new IRST under one wing and a ballasted pod to maintain weight and balance under the opposite wing.

Future enhancements could also include a helmet mounted sight. Integration of a helmet mounted sighting system for off-boresight weapons aiming was initially frustrated due to technical difficulties in 'mapping' the Raptor's cockpit, and by the requirement for extensive software changes, though the Thales Scorpion helmet-mounted cuing system (HMCS) was successfully tested on the F-22 in 2013. Funding cuts (and perhaps aspirations for a more sophisticated helmet) delayed its deployment, but the new R1 architecture may provide an opportunity to integrate one of three commercial-off-the-shelf helmets now understood to be under evaluation.

Planned navigation system upgrades aim to ensure the F-22's ability to maintain its precision attack, navigation, and timing capabilities in GPS-degraded environments.

Supporters say that the F-22 cannot be matched by any known or projected fighter aircraft, raising the question as to why the Next Generation Air Dominance (NGAD) fighter is

needed at all, and whether just putting the F-22 back into production would not be a better idea. But this argument has been lost, and the F-22's fate has been sealed. However, in the meantime, F-22s have been used to evaluate

equipment and systems for NGAD, and the USAF may leverage some of this technology for Raptor upgrades. While it does remain in service, the F-22 will certainly continue to 'rule the roost'. ∎

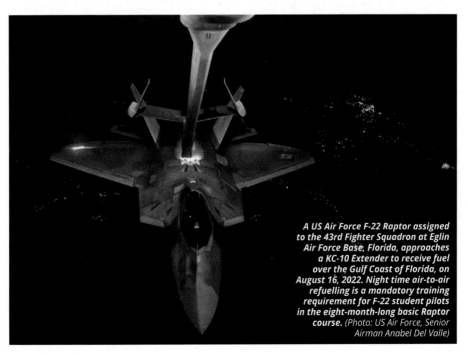

A US Air Force F-22 Raptor assigned to the 43rd Fighter Squadron at Eglin Air Force Base, Florida, approaches a KC-10 Extender to receive fuel over the Gulf Coast of Florida, on August 16, 2022. Night time air-to-air refuelling is a mandatory training requirement for F-22 student pilots in the eight-month-long basic Raptor course. (Photo: US Air Force, Senior Airman Anabel Del Valle)

This F-15E Strike Eagle wears the MO tail codes and tiger striped fin markings of the 366th Fighter Wing's 391st Fighter Squadron but was probably temporarily assigned to an expeditionary when photographed approaching the tanker during a mission in the US Central Command area of responsibility on January 27, 2021. The WSO in the back seat appears to be photographing the photographer! (Photo: US Air Force, Staff Sgt Sean Carnes)

McDonnell Douglas F-15E Strike Eagle

In August 2008, an F-15E became the first USAF fighter to fly powered by a blend of synthetic fuel and JP-8. But the Strike Eagle is not defined by its environmental credentials, but rather by its war-fighting capability.

The 'Mudhen' (as the F-15E Strike Eagle is fondly known to its aircrews) is arguably the most proficient multi-role, air-to-air and air-to-ground strike fighter in the USAF inventory, ranging further and carrying more weapons than its rivals. But despite being probably the most 'in demand' tactical aircraft type, the F-15E Strike

Eagle fleet is facing a significant reduction in size by the end of the decade. The air force plans to cut 119 of its 218 F-15Es by Fiscal Year 2028, phasing out those aircraft powered by the 23,500lb st Pratt & Whitney F100-PW-220E turbofan engine, while retaining only those powered by the 29,000lb st F100-PW-229. These engines now

incorporate an advanced digital electronic engine control system which allows them to accelerate from idle power to maximum afterburner in less than four seconds, a 40% improvement over the previous engine control system.

Apart from its monochrome dark grey paint job and conformal fuel tanks, the F-15E looks

The F-15E has always had a formidable air-to-air capability, and this was exercised from the start. Here two F-15Es from the 90th Fighter Squadron, Elmendorf AFB, Alaska, fire a pair of AIM-7M's during a training mission. The mission took place over the Gulf of Mexico just off the coast of Florida. (Photo: US Air Force, Major Gary)

much the same as any two-seat Eagle, but the similarities are largely skin deep – limited to the overall size, shape, and configuration of the aircraft. Inside the 'outer mould line' the F-15D and the F-15E are very different aircraft. Each of the low-drag conformal fuel tanks carried by the F-15E can carry 750 gallons of fuel but incorporate short low-drag weapons that further extend the range of the Strike Eagle.

Whereas the F-15C is all about air superiority, and the F-15D is its two-seat trainer variant, the F-15E Strike Eagle is a two-seat multi-role tactical fighter designed to perform both air-to-air and air-to-ground missions by day or night, and in all weather conditions.

The F-15E is a dual-role fighter, designed to be able to fight its way to a target over long ranges, destroy enemy targets, and then fight its way out. As such the type is capable of deep interdiction and tactical nuclear strike missions but is also a powerful and agile fighter capable

of sustaining 9g throughout the flight envelope with the same weapons as the F-15C, but with an arguably better radar! In recent years, it has proved equally adept at Close Air Support, prosecuting fleeting, and time sensitive targets with precision guided munitions.

Even in 2023, with large numbers of F-35As in service, the F-15E remains the USAF's tactical fighter of choice across a range of mission sets.

Strike Eagle history

The basic F-15 Eagle always had considerable air-to-ground potential, but the USAF was determined that its new fighter would be a 'pure' air superiority fighter. Its job was to 'Kill Migs', and nothing was going to be allowed to dilute this. "Not a pound for air to ground," the F-15 Special Project Office insisted.

But while this meant that the F-15 was well suited to replace air defence roled F-106 Delta Darts, and some of the USAF's F-4 Phantoms, ▶

The 28th Test and Evaluation Squadron and 85th Test and Evaluation Squadron executed the first-ever guided launch of the AIM-120D3 Advanced Medium Range Air-to-Air Missile on June 30, 2022, as part of the Form, Fit, Function, Refresh (F3R) programme. This F-15E Strike Eagle used the missile – the latest AMRAAM variant - in successfully engaging a QF-16 full-scale aerial target. (Photo: US Air Force)

An F-15E Strike Eagle assigned to the 492nd Expeditionary Fighter Squadron taxiing out at Bagram Airfield, Afghanistan during the long and ultimately fruitless US involvement. The 492nd EFS was deployed from Lakenheath Air Base, England. (Photo: US Air Force, Staff Sgt Craig Seals)

there was an obvious requirement for a multi role tactical fighter to replace aircraft like the General Dynamics F-111 and the remaining F-4Es. Accordingly, McDonnell Douglas quietly set to create a tactical fighter derivative of the F-15, though there was no formally stated requirement for such an aircraft, nor even any official expressions of interest.

What became the F-15E began life as a fighter bomber derivative of the two-seat F-15B, with the rear cockpit occupied by a WSO who would operate a ground attack optimised weapons delivery system. The WSO had four screens to display information from the radar, LANTIRN, or electronic warfare system, while monitoring aircraft or weapons status. The WSO could monitor possible threats, select targets, and could use an electronic 'moving map' for navigation, using two hand controllers to select new displays or to refine targeting information. the F-15E's back seat is equipped with its own stick and throttle allowing the WSO to fly the aircraft if required.

The redesigned F-15E airframe was built with a stronger structure allowing heavier take-off weights and double the service life compared to the original F-15 Eagle. The aft fuselage in particular was redesigned to accommodate more powerful engines with advanced engine bay structures and doors, which incorporated Superplastic forming and diffusion bonding technologies.

The USAF initiated the Tactical All-Weather Requirement Study In 1978. This looked at a range of options, including the McDonnell Douglas proposal. The study eventually recommended adoption of the F-15E as the USAF's future strike platform.

To assist in the development of the definitive F-15E, McDonnell Douglas modified the second TF-15A prototype, 71-0291, to serve as the Advanced Fighter Capability Demonstrator, flying in its new guise on July 8, 1980. It had previously been used to assess conformal fuel tanks (CFTs), initially designed for the F-15 as 'FAST Packs', with FAST standing for 'Fuel and Sensor, Tactical. It was subsequently fitted with a Pave Tack laser designator pod to allow it to self-designate when dropping laser guided bombs. McDonnell Douglas used a number of other F-15s to support the programme, including 78-0468, 80-0055, and 81-0063.

The USAF announced its Enhanced Tactical Fighter requirement for a replacement for the F-111 in March 1981, later renaming the programme as the Dual-Role Fighter (DRF) competition and outlining an eventual requirement for 392 aircraft. The USAF wanted an aircraft that would be capable of flying deep penetration air interdiction missions without fighter escort or EW support. McDonnell Douglas submitted the new F-15E, and in February 1984 this aircraft prevailed over the rival big wing General Dynamics F-16XL. The

Strike Eagle promised lower development costs, better growth potential, and twin-engine redundancy.

The F-15E was based on the Hughes AN/APG-70 multi-mode radar – a 1980s redesign of the APG-63 with greater reliability, easier maintenance, and additional modes. The APG-70 radar system allowed near-simultaneous air-to-air and air-to-ground operation. After a sweep of a target area, the crew could 'freeze' the resulting air-to-ground map while the radar then went back into the air-to-air mode allowing the pilot to detect, target and engage air-to-air targets while the weapons systems officer (WSO) designated the ground target for air-to-surface weapons delivery.

The F-15E augmented its radar with the LANTIRN (low-altitude navigation and targeting infrared for night) system. This consisted of two pods – the AN/AAQ-13 navigation pod with terrain-following radar for navigation and the AN/AAQ-14 targeting pod with a high-resolution, forward looking infrared sensor and a laser rangefinder/designator. The navigation pod's terrain following radar could present cues in the pilot's head-up display (HUD) or could be coupled to the autopilot to provide 'hands off' terrain-following capability. The targeting pod could display its video picture projected on the pilot's head-up display, providing an infrared image of the ground.

LANTIRN allowed the F-15E to be flown at low altitudes, at night and in any weather, and to attack ground targets with unequalled accuracy using a variety of precision-guided and unguided weapons. Latterly, the AN/AAQ-14 targeting pod (mounted beneath the left engine intake) has been replaced by the AN/AAQ-28 LITENING Targeting Pod, or the AN/AAQ-33 Sniper Advanced Targeting Pod.

McDonnell Douglas began construction of three initial F-15Es in July 1985. The first of these had the full F-15E avionics suite and the redesigned front fuselage and flew on December 11, 1986. The second aircraft added the redesigned aft fuselage and the common engine bay, and the third, which flew on March 31, 1987, incorporated all the changes and was a full standard F-15E.

The first of 236 production Strike Eagles (and not 392 as had once been planned) was handed over to the 461st Tactical Fighter Training Squadron ('Deadly Jesters'), part of the 405th Tactical Training Wing at Luke AFB, on April 12, 1988. The first operational unit — the 4th Tactical Fighter Wing's 336th Tactical Fighter Squadron ('Rocketeers') — received its first Strike Eagles at Seymour Johnson Air Force Base, North Carolina, in December 1988. The F-15E reached initial operational capability with the 336th Tactical Fighter Squadron on September 30, 1989.

The F-15E made its combat debut during Operation Desert Storm in 1991. The 336th Tactical Fighter Squadron flew to Seeb Air Base in Oman while the 335th and 336th squadrons deployed to Prince Sultan Air Base in Saudi Arabia, close to Iraq's border. Some 24 F-15Es launched an attack on five fixed Scud installations in western Iraq on January 17, 1991, at the start of Operation Desert Storm

1st Lt Kyle Gager, a 492nd Fighter Squadron weapons systems officer, steps out of the cockpit of an F-15E Strike Eagle during an Agile Combat Employment exercise at RAF Fairford, England, on August 23, 2021. Using ACE concepts ensures that US forces in Europe are better equipped to operate from locations with varying levels of capacity and support. (Photo: US Air Force, Senior Airman Eugene Oliver)

and by night they flew Scud-hunting missions over the region.

On the opening night of the war, F-15Es engaged a lone MiG-29 with AIM-9 Sidewinders. The enemy aircraft was eventually brought down by a missile of unknown origin.

An F-15E was lost to enemy fire during a strike against a petrol oil and lubricant plant near Basra, on January 18, killing both crew. This mission was described as having been the most difficult and dangerous of the war as the

target was heavily defended by SA-3, SA-6, SA-8 and Roland SAMs and anti-aircraft artillery. On January 20, a second F-15E was downed by an SA-2; the crew survived and evaded capture for several days, but a rescue was not launched because one of the airmen had failed to identify himself with the correct codes. The Iraqis later captured both crew.

An F-15E scored the type's only air-to-air kill of the war on February 14, using a GBU-10 bomb to down a Mil Mi-24 helicopter flying ▶

Three F-15E Strikes Eagles from the 335th Fighter Squadron return from deployment on October 12, 2016, at Seymour Johnson Air Force Base, North Carolina. The aircraft are led by 89-0487, flown by Lt Col Brandon Johnson. More than ten Strike Eagles returned from an undisclosed location in Southwest Asia where they provided support for Operation Inherent Resolve. (Photo: US Air Force, Airman Shawna L. Keyes)

An F-15E Strike Eagle from the 391st Fighter Squadron drops a GBU-28 during a Combat Hammer mission at Hill Air Force Base, Utah. Twelve aircraft, 18 pilots, and 30 crews from the 391st FS travelled down to Hill AFB to participate in the three week weapons system evaluation. (Photo: US Air Force)

at about 800 feet. The feat was witnessed by US Special Forces.

F-15Es struck heavily defended targets throughout Iraq, prioritising SCUD missile sites, but also flying missions aimed at killing Iraqi President Saddam Hussein, at knocking out enemy armour, and attacking enemy airfields.

Since then, F-15Es have participated in most operations flown by the US Air Force. The F-15E proved to be the only fighter able to attack ground targets around the clock, in all weather conditions during the long-running 1990s Balkan conflict. During Operation Allied Force in 1999, 26 F-15Es flew the first strikes of the war against Serb surface-to-air-missile sites, anti-aircraft batteries and early warning radar stations. Operating from RAF Lakenheath and from Aviano in Italy, F-15Es flew close air support (CAS) missions, carrying a mix of air-to-air and air-to-ground weapons – allowing them to perform both combat air patrol and strike roles in the same mission. These missions typically lasted for around seven and a half hours and included two air-to-air refuelling contacts. The F-15E was frequently armed with the AGM-130, which provided a stand-off strike capability.

Since then, the F-15E has seen action in Afghanistan, Iraq, Syria, and Libya. During Operation Enduring Freedom in Afghanistan four F-15E crews from the 391st Fighter Squadron conducted what was claimed to be the longest fighter mission in history: lasting a total of 15.5 hours and involving 12 air-to-air refuelling contacts. The four F-15Es spent nine of those hours loitering over the target area, attacking Taliban command and control facilities, a road block, and other targets.

During Operation Iraqi Freedom, on April 7, 2003, one F-15E, crewed by Captain Eric Das and Major William Watkins, was shot down by AA fire during an interdiction mission in support of special forces near Tikrit. Both crew were posthumously awarded the Distinguished Flying Cross and the Purple Heart.

Another F-15E was lost during Operation Odyssey Dawn - the allied intervention in Libya. The 492nd Fighter Squadron aircraft crashed near Benghazi on March 21, 2011. The crew experienced a sudden loss of control when the aircraft exceeded the angle of attack limit during a combat egress after dropping a GBU-38 bomb. The crew ejected and were eventually rescued by the US Marine Corps.

USAF F-15Es have participated in Operation Inherent Resolve against the so-called Islamic State (ISIS) insurgents in Iraq and Syria, participating in numerous attacks against a wide variety of targets. The campaign has also provided more opportunities for the F-15E to add to its tally of air-to-air victories. On June 8, 2017, an F-15E shot down a Predator sized UAV near Al Tanf, Syria after the drone deployed 'one of several weapons it was carrying near a position occupied by Coalition personnel'.

Strike Eagle weapons

The F-15E can carry the majority of the air-launched precision-guided and stand-off munitions in the USAF's current inventory, including the joint direct attack munition (JDAM), joint stand-off weapon (JSOW) and the wind-corrected munition dispenser (WCMD). But perhaps most significantly it is the tactical platform of choice for outsized stand-off ➤

A US Air Force F-15E Strike Eagle aircraft from the 391st Expeditionary Fighter Squadron deploys flares during a flight over Afghanistan on November 12, 2008. The squadron was deployed from Mountain Home to Bagram Air Base at the time. (Photo: US Air Force, Staff Sgt Aaron Allmon)

This Eglin-based F-15E was used for trials of the new B61-12 – the latest version of the USAF's standard freefall nuclear weapon. The F-15E completed six drops of the new weapon in March 2020, becoming the first aircraft type in the inventory cleared to use the weapon. (Photo: US Air Force)

An F-15E Strike Eagle from Mountain Home Air Force Base, Idaho, carrying a B61 Joint Test Assembly, departs Nellis Air Force Base, Nevada, for the Tonopah Test Range during DCA NucWSEP. F-15Es released B61-3 and B61-4 JTAs to further test the F-15E's inherent ability to deliver B61 series tactical nuclear weapons. (Photo Courtesy US Air Force, Santos Torres)

A pair of heritage painted F-15E Strike Eagles assigned to the 48th Fighter Wing manoeuvre over southern England on June 9, 2019, wearing markings intended to evoke those worn by P-47 Thunderbolts during World War Two. (Photo: US Air Force, Tech Sgt Matthew Plew)

strike weapons that cannot be carried by the USAF's stealthy tactical aircraft. An F-15E conducted the first test-drop of the 5,000lb GBU-72 Advanced 5K Penetrator on October 7, 2021. This was probably the heaviest weapon ever to be carried by a tactical fast jet combat aircraft. The Strike Eagle has conducted demonstration flights carrying five AGM-158 JASSM missiles or ferrying up to 15 JDAMs to forward airfields.

The F-15E is also the platform of choice for the new B61-12 tactical nuclear gravity bomb. The F-15E was the first jet certified to employ this latest variant of the B61, making an initial drop on June 8, 2020. And at the other end of the size and lethality spectrum, the F-15E is also cleared to carry the Raytheon GBU-53/B SDB II StormBreaker, following a series of test drops which began on September 23, 2020.

For self-defence, the F-15E also can be armed with the AIM-9M Sidewinder or AIM-120 AMRAAM (advanced medium range air-to-air missile) for the air-to-air role, while the internally mounted 20mm M61A1 Gatling gun has up to 500 20mm rounds for use against airborne targets, or for strafe.

A 53rd Wing F-15E completed the first-ever guided launch of the new AIM-120D3 variant using production missile hardware on June 30, 2022, successfully engaging a QF-16 full-scale aerial target. The test was conducted by the 28th Test and Evaluation Squadron and the

'Cerberus' is an F-15E Strike Eagle assigned to the 391st Fighter Squadron at Mountain Home but is seen here departing the tanker after receiving fuel over the US Central Command area of responsibility, on March 17, 2021. Interestingly, the back seater seems to be wearing JHMCS, while the pilot does not. (Photo: US Air Force, Staff Sgt Taylor Harrison)

85th TES and executed a long-range shot that physically stressed the new missile hardware and verified missile performance capabilities.

The AMRAAM AIM-120D3 was developed under the AMRAAM Form, Fit, Function Refresh (F3R) programme. In the months preceding the launch, the test team conducted several captive-carry test missions with AIM-120D3 instrumented test vehicles to collect data and ensure the new missile hardware and software functioned correctly.

Today's F-15E is a much more capable and advanced aircraft than the F-15Es deployed to fight the so-called Islamic State (ISIS), or even those used over Libya in 2011. Sniper, and Litening Advanced Targeting pods have supplanted LANTIRN, and the JHMCS helmet mounted cueing system is in frontline use.

The old legacy AN/APG-70 mechanically scanned radar has given way to the new APG-82(V)1 AESA active electronically scanned array radar. The AN/APG-82 combines the processor of the APG-79 (used on the F/A-18E/F Super Hornet) with the antenna of the APG-63(V)3 AESA now fitted to the F-15C, and, in conjunction with a new wideband radome, provides a massive boost in capability. The first APG-82 test radar was delivered to Boeing in 2010, beginning flight tests that January. Frontline Strike Eagle squadrons were starting to operate with the new radar by 2017, providing significantly expanded mission employment capabilities.

Upgraded cockpit display processors and AESA-compatible large-area digital displays will allow F-15E aircrew to fully exploit the capabilities of the new radar, while MIDS/JTRS and a new BLOS Satcom will enable higher capacity, jam-resistant Link 16 communications and data transfer.

The F-15E is receiving the new BAE Systems Eagle Passive/Active Warning Survivability System (EPAWSS), which promises to bring defensive, situational awareness, and electronic attack improvements, replacing the original Northrop Grumman Tactical Electronic Warfare System self-protection suite, which is 'functionally obsolete' and costly to sustain.

In March 2021, BAE Systems announced that it had begun low-rate initial production of EPAWSS for the F-15E under a $58m subcontract from Boeing. An initial two US Air Force F-15E aircraft received Eagle Passive Active Warning and Survivability System

(EPAWSS) modifications in 2022, and Boeing said that the air force plans to equip 43 of the service's F-15Es with EPAWSS (having earlier said that all 217 survivors would be so equipped).

The air force has said that EPAWSS will significantly improve the F-15E's ability to counter radio frequency, electro-optical, and infrared threats in highly contested environments keeping the aircraft viable through to 2040. It has been estimated that installing EPAWSS on all F-15Es could cost $2.7bn for Increment 1 and Increment 2 thereafter. Increment 1 replaces the existing radar warning receiver, internal countermeasure system and countermeasure dispenser system, while Increment 2 will add a towed decoy and monopulse angle countermeasures capability.

EPAWSS is also planned for the US Air Force's F-15EX Eagle II fighters, and the first F-15EX test aircraft with EPAWSS debuted the system in Exercise Northern Edge in May, 2021. "The first two F-15EX aircraft, delivered ahead of schedule, participated in exercises with the EPAWSS suite. During the highly contested and complex exercises, the two jets demonstrated operational potential, which set the stage for future incremental improvements, allowing the jets to exhibit proven, outstanding performance in subsequent exercises and flight test missions in October, 2021 and February, 2022," Boeing said.

The F-15E's Operational Flight Program software is transitioning to an annual update cycle that will allow the integration of new mission capabilities more quickly, probably ▶

A 332nd Air Expeditionary Wing F-15E Strike Eagle conducts a sortie during a routine training exercise at an undisclosed location in Southwest Asia, July 6, 2022, dropping live weapons on the range. (Photo: US Air Force, Master Sgt Kelly Goonan)

in tandem with the F-15C/D and F-15EX. A replacement Data Transfer Module promises to improve flight planning and debrief, while other future enhancements are expected to include a new Mobile User Objective System (MUOS) secure, jam-resistant SATCOM and NATO-interoperable SATURN UHF. The aircraft is also expected to be equipped with the Legion Pod IRST for passive detection, tracking and engagement of air targets.

Squadrons

Today, the F-15E equips four squadrons of the 4th Fighter Wing at Seymour Johnson AFB, North Carolina. These are the 333rd Fighter Squadron 'Lancers', the 334th Fighter Squadron 'Eagles', the 335th Fighter Squadron 'Chiefs', and the 336th Fighter Squadron 'Rocketeers'.

The 944th Fighter Wing, headquartered at Luke AFB, Arizona, is the Air Force Reserve's largest F-16, A-10, F-15E, and F-35 training wing, and trains F-16, F-15E, F-35, and A-10 pilots for the United States Air Force, Air Force Reserve, Air National Guard, and parents a geographically separated unit at Seymour Johnson Air Force Base.

The 366th Fighter Wing at Mountain Home AFB, Idaho includes the 389th Fighter Squadron 'Thunderbolts' and the 391st Fighter Squadron 'Bold Tigers' as well as the 428th Fighter Squadron – a mixed USAF/RSAF training unit flying the F-15SG. The 'Bold Tigers' at least operate later block F-15Es powered by the F100-PW-229 engine, as do both UK-based squadrons.

The 48th Fighter Wing at RAF Lakenheath, includes the 492nd Fighter Squadron 'Mad Hatters' and the 494th Fighter Squadron 'Panthers', which operate alongside two squadrons of F-35As.

The 219-strong, six frontline squadron Strike Eagle fleet remains in high demand – and maintains an enduring commitment in the US Central Command region that ensures that at least one squadron is always deployed.

During one deployment, which ended in May 2020, F-15E Strike Eagles of the 389th Fighter Squadron, from Mountain Home Air Force Base, Idaho are believed to have fired stealthy AGM-158 Joint Air-to-Surface Standoff Missiles (JASSM) as part of the raid that killed ISIS founder Abu Bakr Al Baghdadi in October 2019. The 389th were operating from Muwaffaq Salti Air Base in Jordan.

The F-15E has continued to add to its laurels, taking on new responsibilities and practising new and/or unfamiliar roles.

During Exercise Atlantic Thunder 22 in September 2022, the former-USS *Boone*, a decommissioned Oliver Hazard Perry-class frigate, was the target for a SINKEX. Among the attacking aircraft were F-15Es from the 494th Fighter Squadron, based at RAF Lakenheath, which dropped several Joint Direct Attack Munitions (JDAMs) on the ship. A Boeing P-8 Poseidon from VP-46 fired a Harpoon at the vessel, while Typhoons from the RAF's No.41 Squadron attacked the ship with Paveway IV bombs, and a Wildcat HMA2 helicopter from 815 Naval Air Squadron, used its MX-15HDi electro-optical/infrared sensor turret to provide targeting support – and fired Martlet missiles at the ship.

The exercise followed an earlier trial in the Gulf of Mexico in April 2022, when an F-15E Strike Eagle sank a retired cargo ship (the *Courageous*) using a new 'Quicksink' version of the 2,000lb Joint Direct Attack Munition. The Quicksink is fused to explode immediately below its target ship, lifting it out of the water and breaking it in half.

With the withdrawal of the F-15C from USAFE, the F-15Es of the 492nd Fighter Squadron at RAF Lakenheath began conducting deterrence operations at Łask Air Base, Poland, on November 29, 2022, in support of the US forward fighter presence along NATO's eastern flank. The F-15Es flew in a new configuration, without their usual conformal fuel tanks (CFTs). Their removal was intended to improve the Strike Eagle's air dominance capabilities, reportedly allowing them to supercruise, and enhancing the type's agility.

The F-15E force has also picked up a new responsibility supporting PACAF. Following the withdrawal of the F-15C/Ds from Kadena Air Base, Japan, F-15Es have already begun making rotational deployments to 'plug the gap'.

F-22 Raptors from Joint Base Elmendorf-Richardson, Alaska and F-16 Fighting Falcons from Spangdahlem Air Force Base, Germany, were the first two sets of aircraft to begin the rotational presence at Kadena in place of the F-15C permanent squadrons, but in early April were themselves relieved by F-15Es from the 336th Fighter Squadron at Seymour Johnson Air Force Base, and, from late April 2023, by the F-15Es of the 391st Fighter Squadron from Mountain Home Air Force Base, Idaho. Meanwhile, F-15Es remain extremely active in Centcom. On March 23, 2023, just hours after an Iranian drone struck a military base housing US troops near Hasakah in northeast Syria, killing a US contractor and injuring five US servicemen and a second US contractor, Central Command (CENTCOM) dispatched F-15Es to

Laden with weapons, a Strike Eagle from the 494th Fighter Squadron taxis in to park at Al Dhafra Air Base, United Arab Emirates, on October 18, 2019. The 494th FS 'Panthers' deployed from the 48th Fighter Wing, at Royal Air Force Lakenheath, England, joining a diverse fleet of F-35A Lightning IIs, KC-10 Extenders, E-3 Sentrys, and RQ-4 Global Hawks to support operations in the region. (Photo: US Air Force, Tech Sgt Kat Justen)

An F-15E Strike Eagle of the 4th Fighter Wing at Seymour Johnson Air Force Base, North Carolina flies near a rainbow over the southeastern United States on August 8, 2018. The Strike Eagle had just been refuelled by a KC-135 Stratotanker of the 121st Air Refueling Wing, Ohio. (Photo: US Air National Guard, Airman 1st Class Tiffany A. Emery)

launch retaliatory strikes against Iranian IRGC and affiliated targets in Syria.

It is unclear what will replace the F-15Es, as they are retired. It is not even apparent what will replace the Kadena F-15Cs, as orders for the F-15EX do not seem sufficient to replace these as well as the remaining ANG F-15Cs. Nor would F-35A production rates seem adequate to replace the F-15Es in the required timescale.

A USAF Justification and Approval (J&A) document noted that the objective of the F-15EX programme was: "to rapidly develop, integrate, and field the F-15EX weapon system to refresh/replace aging F-15C/D aircraft. A decision to also refresh F-15E aircraft has not yet been made but remains an option."

It explained that: "The F-15 fleet is in dire need of a refresh, in particular the F-15C/D fleet, which without an expensive service life extension, will run out of airframe flying hours in [date redacted]." The need to replace the Strike Eagle will become just as urgent as it is now for the F-15C/D.

Procuring additional F-15EX Eagle IIs to recapitalise the F-15E fleet would make a great deal of sense. Maintaining F-15EX production would make it much easier for the USAF to acquire 72 fighters annually – and thereby recapitalise the overall fighter fleet at the required rate. The J&A report stressed the ease of transition to the new Eagle variant: "Refreshing the existing F-15 fleet (versus

A US Air Force pilot sits in the cockpit of an F-15E Strike Eagle aircraft during an integrated combat turn exercise at Al Udeid Air Base, Qatar, on March 3, 2021. The ICT training allowed airmen to rehearse the rapid deployment capabilities of aircraft within the US Central Command area of responsibility. (Photo: US Air Force, Tech Sgt Brigette Waltermire)

transitioning to a new advanced fighter aircraft) with F-15EX will dramatically reduce disruption to the logistics and sustainment infrastructure, as well as operational training and Mission

Ready status of current F-15 units, by taking advantage of inherent familiarity with the existing aircraft, which will allow focus on the new and improved systems." ∎

'Fleet Leader'

Since the F-15E fleet is arguably the most hard-worked in the air force, it should perhaps come as no surprise that it was a Strike Eagle that became the first of the family to clock up 10,000 flying hours, and then 12,000.

McDonnell Douglas F-15E-47-MC Strike Eagle 89-0487 is probably the most distinguished airframe in the fleet. On Valentine's Day, 1991 89-0487 still had that 'new car smell' when its crew, Captains Tim Bennett and Dan Bakke, used a 2,000lb GBU-10 Paveway II laser-guided bomb to 'shoot down' a low-flying Iraqi Mil Mi-24 Hind attack helicopter.

Captain Rick Bennett (pilot) and Captain Daniel Bakke (weapons systems officer) were leading a two-ship flight of Strike Eagles on an anti-Scud missile patrol, waiting for a target to be assigned by the controller on 'their' Boeing E-3 Sentry AWACS aircraft. 89-0487 was carrying four laser-guided GBU-10 bombs and four AIM-9 Sidewinder heat-seeking air-to-air missiles. Bennett's wingman was carrying 12 Mk.82 500lb bombs.

The controller called Bennett's flight and told them that a Special Forces team on the ground had been located by Iraqi forces while searching for Scud launching sites and needed air support. The two F-15Es descended though a thick 12,000ft layer of clouds, popping out into the clear at 2,500ft and about 15–20 miles from the Special Forces team. Bennett used the Strike Eagle's LANTIRN navigation pod to survey the scene and saw that five enemy Mi-24s helicopters were landing troops to drive the US troops towards a pre-positioned Iraqi blocking force.

Dan Bakke aimed the LANTIRN laser designator at the lead Iraqi helicopter and

The mission scoreboard on the nose of 89-0487 included a green star marking its Desert Storm kill, and rows of arrows and tomahawks marking individual missions – befitting an aircraft assigned to a squadron known as the 'Chiefs'. (Photo: US Air Force, Airman 1st Class Ericka Engblom)

prepared to drop a GBU-10 while Bennett busied himself preparing to fire a Sidewinder missile if the helicopter lifted off. Four miles out, Bakke released a GBU-10, but the enemy helicopter began to climb and accelerate.

Bakke kept the laser locked on what became a relatively fast-moving target, however, and scored a hit on the Mi-24, which disintegrated.

The other four enemy helicopters scattered. Further coalition fighter bombers arrived

F-15E Strike Eagle 89-0487 taxies out at Bagram Airfield, Afghanistan, on January 13, 2012. 89-0487 was the first F-15E to score an air-to-air kill and is seen here with a green star commemorating that achievement. The aircraft also wears the original 'Eagle Squadron' markings from World War Two, including an RAF-type crest on the intake. (Photo: US Air Force, Airman 1st Class Ericka Engblom)

Senior Airman 'Bradley' and Lt Colonel Brandon Johnson, 335th Expeditionary Fighter Squadron commander, apply a 12,000 flying hour decal to the side of F-15E Strike Eagle 89-0487 after its milestone flight on August 16, 2016. Johnson also achieved a career milestone of 3,000 flying hours after 25 years of service during the same flight. (Photo: US Air Force, Staff Sgt Samantha Mathison)

on scene to defend the US Special Forces team, who were safely extracted and who subsequently confirmed Bakke's remarkable kill.

By 2012, 89-0487 was the flagship of the 335th Expeditionary Flying Squadron, operating from Bagram Airfield, in Afghanistan, and bearing the names of Lt Col David Moeller, 335th Expeditionary Flying Squadron commander and senior WSO, and his pilot on its nose. By then the aircraft had participated in operations Desert Storm, Deliberate Guard, Northern Watch, Southern Watch, Iraqi Freedom, and Enduring Freedom, and had 8,800 hours 'on the clock' when it arrived in Afghanistan. Three months later, it was on the verge of reaching 10,000 flying hours, having dropped 15% of all bombs released by the squadron.

As his own personal nod to history, Moeller chose to pass the honour of flying 89-0487 on the mission that would take it past 10,000 hours to the youngest pilot and WSO on the squadron. Thus, it was Capt Ryan Bodenheimer, pilot, and Capt Erin Short, weapons systems officer who flew the aircraft on its historic mission on January 13, 2012.

"It just seemed appropriate that the longest flying F-15E be flown by the youngest flyers in the unit," Moeller later explained.

By August 2016, 89-0487 was known as 'America's Jet' and had deployed 17 times in

Colonel Brandon Johnson, 335th Expeditionary Fighter Squadron commander, climbs down from 89-0487 after the squadron's return to Seymour Johnson. (Photo: US Air Force, Staff Sgt Samantha Mathison)

support of combat operations. The mount of Col Brandon Johnson, 335th Expeditionary Fighter Squadron commander, during an Operation Inherent Resolve sortie, the aircraft became the first to achieve 12,000 flying hours on August 16, 2016. Johnson reached 3,000 flying hours on the same sortie, after 25 years of service.

"All of our aircraft have different temperaments, so to speak, but America's Jet consistently outperforms all of our other jets," MSgt Richard, 380th EAMXS lead production superintendent said. "We work hard to keep our aircraft in the air, so the 12,000 hour milestone is a testament to all of the maintainers who've kept her flying. That's why we call her America's Jet; because she is full of grit and fortitude, the embodiment of the American spirit, and has demonstrated this in every major conflict since Desert Storm."

In 2018, Lt Col Isaac Bell, the then commander of the 335th, said that 89-0487 had been responsible for another air-to-air kill – presumably meaning one of the two Iranian-built Shahed 129 drones shot down near at-Tanf in Syria on June 8 and June 20, 2017. Unfortunately, while this would have been a great addition to the story, it seems that the colonel was mistaken. The two drone kills were scored by 97-0219 and 98-0135 of the 492nd Fighter Squadron, deployed to CENTCOM from RAF Lakenheath.

Boeing F-15EX Eagle II

An F-15EX Eagle II Fighter Jet assigned to the 40th Flight Test Squadron, prepares to take off at Nellis Air Force Base, Nevada, on October 20, 2021. Both of the air force's F-15EX aircraft were at Nellis AFB to conduct test and training missions to determine how effective and suitable the aircraft was for its air-to-air mission.
(Photo: US Air Force, William R. Lewis)

America's newest fighter, the F-15EX, also happens to be a derivative of its oldest – an aircraft that entered service almost 50 years ago.

The USAF in 2023 is not the USAF that was planned back in the heady days of the Cold War. Then, the USAF expected that it would one day field an 'all stealth' combat aircraft force – based on the Northrop B-2, and on Lockheed's F-117, F-22 and F-35. Cost constraints and the rise of stealthy stand-off weapons led to a more realistic bomber mix, but the air force remained wedded to the idea that it would only procure low observable (stealthy) fifth-generation fighter aircraft, phasing out fourth-generation fighters like the F-15 and F-16 as quickly as it could replace them.

The USAF fully expected that, over a 25 year period, it would have replaced its entire fighter inventory with F-22 Raptors and F-35 Lightning IIs - thereby fielding an all-stealth fighter force. (And, just so you know, it had planned to do much the same with its bomber fleet, procuring 132 B-2s).

The plans to field an all-stealth fighter fleet were dealt a serious blow when F-22 production was scaled back from 750 aircraft to 187; and then another by the multitude of problems that held up full rate production of the F-35. The

programme of record for the F-35 remains at 1,760 aircraft, but deliveries will be stretched out over several decades, meaning that the USAF will be forced to rely on the non-stealthy, fourth-generation fighters it was so keen to get rid of. These ageing 'fourth-gen' aircraft would have to 'soldier on' for far longer than had ever been planned.

And it's actually worse than that. The USAF soon realised that it could not simply phase out its existing fighters as new F-35As rolled off the production line to replace them. Production of the new could never keep pace with the need to replace the old – or not at anything like the rate required. If it were to keep force levels at anything like the required size, the USAF would actually have to buy more new-build fourth-generation fighters.

Fortunately, the USAF soon came to realise the value of operating fourth- and fifth-generation aircraft together to provide a more lethal and cost-effective force than would be possible by using fifth-generation platforms alone. With the right datalinks and tactics, the distinct advantages of each generation could

be leveraged, while at the same time avoiding or mitigating against the inherent design weaknesses of either generation.

While fifth-generation platforms like the F-35 can use stealth and advanced sensors to operate within contested airspace, aircraft like the F-15 offer higher performance and large external weapons payloads. In contested regions, teaming F-15Cs with fifth-generation aircraft can make the most out of both platforms. A combined force incorporating both generations is more lethal and cost-effective and will create more complex problems for adversaries attempting to defend against it.

But if the USAF needed more fourth-generation fighters, where would it turn? Buying fighters from its allies was politically unsustainable, even though aircraft like the Eurofighter Typhoon and Dassault Rafale were technically and operationally superior to the much older F-15, F-16, and F/A-18.

With Lockheed Martin struggling to keep up with F-35 production, this ruled out the F-16. This was before the Block 70 had been

Boeing had merged with McDonnell Douglas in August 1997, and oversaw production of the last batches of F-15Es for the USAF (the final delivery taking place in 2002). But that was not the end for the F-15, and Boeing continued to develop and sell the aircraft to export customers, using the two-seat F-15E airframe as the basis of all new export variants. Boeing's marketing efforts continued the patient work of McDonnell Douglas flight operations director Joseph Dobronski, who had demonstrated the aircraft with dozens of potential customers in the back seat. Boeing's own marketing ▶

The F-15SE Silent Eagle mock-up was based on the airframe of a redundant F-15E development aircraft. Stealth modifications included conformal weapons bays and canted tailfins. (Photo: Boeing)

On July 13, 2020 the Department of the Air Force awarded a nearly $1.2bn contract for its first lot of eight F-15EX fighter aircraft. The contract, awarded to Boeing, provides for the design, development, integration, manufacturing, test, verification, certification, delivery, sustainment, and modification of F-15EX aircraft, including spares, support equipment, training materials, technical data, and technical support. (Photo: US Air Force)

launched, and before a new F-16 production line had been established at Greenville.

This left the F-15.

This was perhaps fortuitous, as the premature termination of the F-22 in 2009, had left a significant shortfall in air superiority fighters (a role for which the F-16, and indeed the F-35 are arguably less well suited). The USAF therefore continued to operate a significant fleet of legacy F-15C/D aircraft - primarily from six CONUS-based Air National Guard installations and two active-duty bases at Lakenheath in the UK and Kadena in Japan.

The F-15 was still entirely viable in the CONUS-based air defence role, and the driver for replacing the type was the fact that the available airframes were wearing out, and not because the type itself was no longer capable of conducting the mission. A new-build F-15 would therefore represent an excellent potential gap-filler.

The first F-15EX (20-0001, known as EX1) made its maiden flight at St. Louis' Lambert Field on February 2, 2021 in the hands of Boeing's F-15 chief test pilot Matt 'Phat' Giese and fellow test pilot Mike 'Houdini' Quintini. (Photo: Boeing)

The US Air Force's newest fighter, the F-15EX Eagle II, was revealed and named during a ceremony at Eglin Air Force Base, Florida, on April 8, 2021. The aircraft will be the first US Air Force type to be tested and fielded from beginning to end, through combined developmental and operational tests. (Photo: US Air Force, Samuel King Jr.)

efforts have culminated in 108 recent Eagle sales to Saudi Arabia and Qatar, and these sales have in turn contributed to some $5bn of investment in the development of ever more advanced models of the F-15.

The F-15K Slam Eagle for Korea had an advanced APG-63(V)1 mechanically scanned array radar, an AN/AAS-42 Infra-red search and track system, a customised Tactical Electronics Warfare Suite, and a Joint Helmet Mounted Cueing System. It was also cleared to carry long range standoff weapons including the AGM-84K SLAM-ER, AGM-84H Harpoon Block II, and KEPD 350.

The F-15SG for the Republic of Singapore Air Force was similar but added the AN/APG-63(V)3 AESA radar, and BAE Systems DEWS (Digital Electronic Warfare System), and was armed with AIM-120C and AIM-9X air-to-air

missiles and GBU-38 JDAM and AGM-154 JSOW air-to-ground weapons. These variants kept the F-15 'in the game' and formed the basis of a new generation of so-called 'Advanced Eagle' variants.

Showing an admirable degree of forward-thinking and technological ambition, Boeing produced the F-15SE Silent Eagle concept, first unveiled in March 2009. This added some 'fifth-generation' features to the F-15, including some radar-absorbent material and internal weapons carriage using conformal weapons bays (CWB) instead of conformal fuel tanks, and with the twin vertical tails canted outwards by 15° to reduce radar cross section. The Silent Eagle failed to find a buyer, but some of the less visually obvious features developed for the type did form the basis of the next 'Advanced Eagles'.

The first F-15EX, EX1, arrived at Eglin Air Force Base, Florida on March 11, 2021. The 40th Flight Test Squadron and the 85th Test and Evaluation Squadron personnel are responsible for testing the aircraft. (Photo: US Air Force, Samuel King Jr.)

EX2, assigned to the 85th Test and Evaluation Squadron, 53rd Wing, took flight from Eglin Air Force Base, Florida, for the first time on April 26, 2021, prior to departure for Exercise Northern Edge 2021. The F-15EX brings next-generation combat technology to the highly successful Eagle airframe, enabling it to continue to project power for the joint force. (Photo: US Air Force, 1st Lt Savanah Bray)

Advanced Eagles

The first 'Advanced Eagle' was the F-15SA, developed for the Royal Saudi Air Force, a multi-role fighter aircraft, designed to be built and flown as a two-seater, with a pilot in the front cockpit and a WSO in the rear. The F-15SA included the APG-63(v)3 active electronically scanned array (AESA) radar, digital electronic warfare system (DEWS), and infrared search and track (IRST) systems of the F-15SG and introduced a redesigned fully-digital cockpit (once intended for the F-15SE) and a new fly-by-wire flight control system (FCS) in place of the hybrid electronic/mechanical system used by previous F-15 variants. This allowed the carriage of weapons on the previously unused outer wing hardpoints (Stations 1 and 9) but required a massive flight-test and clearance programme.

The next Advanced Eagle was the F-15QA (Qatar Advanced) for Qatar, known locally as the Ababil. The F-15QA introduced a number of significant improvements over the F-15SA, including a structural enhancement and a new cockpit, as well as the Raytheon AN/APG-82(v)1 Active Electronically Scanned Array (AESA) radar and an ADCP II (Advanced Display Core Processor II) mission computer. ▶

Maj Kevin Hand, an F-15EX operational and experimental test pilot with the Air National Guard/Air Force Reserve Test Center, looks over the aircraft forms before a flight from Nellis Air Force Base, Nevada, on October 20, 2021. Hand flew the F-15EX Eagle II to assess its effectiveness and suitability for the air-to-air mission. (Photo: US Air Force, William R. Lewis)

The F-15EX Integrated Test & Evaluation 2021 Test Patch worn by Lt. Col Wes Turner during testing at Nellis Air Force Base, Nevada, in October 2021. *(Photo: US Air Force, William R. Lewis)*

than that of the legacy F-15, and the F-15EX airframe is designed for a service life of 20,000 flight hours – about double that of an F-15C.

The F-15QA also introduced a new Advanced Cockpit System with very high resolution 10x19in Large Area Displays in both cockpits. The very high-resolution colour image quality of the screen allows for very precise targeting, monitoring of the sensors, and mission management. A new low profile HUD is fitted.

Boeing has also said that it would integrate an Elbit Systems anti-jamming systems into the F-15QA.

The existence of the F-15QA meant that Boeing had a fully developed, tried, and tested and mature Eagle variant available at exactly the point that the USAF realised that it needed one. This decision followed the realisation that a replacement would be required for the USAF's legacy F-15C/Ds, which are in urgent need of recapitalisation. Due to insufficient F-22 procurement and F-35 delays, the F-15C/D fleet has continued flying beyond its designed service life, suffering numerous age-related problems as a result, and running an ever-growing risk of structural failure. It was soon understood that re-equipping the F-15C/D units could not wait for the availability of new F-35As, and that a new Eagle variant would provide a quicker route to the much-needed and long awaited recapitalisation of the USAF fighter force.

Such a new F-15 variant promised to plug the gap quickly and easily, boosting the USAF's

Structurally, the F-15QA's wings and nose barrel were completed using Boeing's Full-Size Determinant Assembly (FSDA) production techniques. FSDA eliminates drilling and shimming from assembly by adding fastener holes at the supplier level, significantly reducing rework, and increasing build quality, as well as increasing the life of the platform. The new Advanced F-15 airframe is designed to be more rugged and more maintainable

The second F-15EX, assigned to the 85th Test and Evaluation Squadron, Eglin Air Force Base, Florida, flying behind a KC-135 of the 465th Air Refueling Squadron, Tinker AFB, Oklahoma, on October 15, 2021. The second aircraft wore black and white chequers on its tailfin, with OT tail codes. *(Photo: US Air Force, 2d Lt Mary Begy)*

The first F-15EX, the Air Force's newest fighter aircraft, arrived at Eglin Air Force Base, Florida on March 11, 2021. EX1 wore red diamonds on white fin stripes, and 'ET' tail codes. The sheer size of the F-15 airframe is apparent in this view. (Photo: US Air Force, 1st Lt Karissa Rodriguez)

shrinking force structure, and reinforcing its air defence capabilities without disrupting the larger F-35 procurement initiative.

The USAF approached Boeing to acquire a derivative of the Advanced Eagle, then dubbed F-15X, in early 2017. This proposed USAF F-15X (known as the F-15CX in single-seat form or as the F-15EX in two seat form) combined the advanced features of the F-15SA with an AN/APG-82 AESA radar – as used by the F-15QA and by upgraded F-15E Strike Eagles.

It was realised that the F-15X could use about 70% of the existing Eagle spares inventory and would be compatible with the F-15C/D's existing ground support equipment and infrastructure. Conversion for pilots and groundcrew would be quick and easy, allowing an active duty F-15C unit to convert from the F-15C/D to the F-15X in 12 months, compared to 18 months for the F-35.

In 2018, the USAF and Boeing briefly discussed procurement of the proposed single-seat F-15CX variant to replace its F-15Cs. This had some appeal, but the single-seat F-15 has been out of production for years, and the USAF instead opted for the two-seat F-15EX. It intends to operate these primarily as single seaters in the pure air defence role, with the second seat facilitating conversion and training, and perhaps enabling future mission expansion. A WSO would be particularly useful for more complex missions – for example when controlling 'Loyal Wingman' UAVs. Although the F-15EX could also allow today's F-15C/D units to embrace a multi-role mission rather than the pure air-to-air role that they have traditionally been assigned, this has not been suggested and is not currently planned.

The F-15EX is not expected to be survivable against modern air defences by 2028 and is planned to be complementary to fifth-generation, stealthy F-35s and F-22s and the new NGAD.

Initially the F-15EX will replace the legacy F-15C/D in the CONUS air defence role, perhaps later flying airbase defence and no-fly zone enforcement missions. The aircraft might even be used to support advanced

fifth-generation fighters operating in more highly contested environments, perhaps bringing larger numbers of air to air weapons to the fight, or perhaps carrying stand-off air-to-ground weapons that are too large to be carried internally by the stealthy jets. These might include HAWC hypersonic missiles or new very long range air-to-air missiles that could be too large for a stealth aircraft's internal bays. The F-15EX could also function ➤

EX2 flying from Eglin Air Force Base, Florida on April 26, 2021, prior to departing for exercise Northern Edge 2021. The USAF is procuring too few F-15EX aircraft to even replace the F-15C one-for-one, but many hope that procurement will be expanded to allow it to replace some of the F-15Es as well as the C-models. (Photo: US Air Force, 1st Lt Savanah Bray)

Lt Col Richard Turner, 40th Flight Test Squadron commander, wears a JHMCS (Joint Helmet Mounted Cueing System) helmet as he taxies the F-15EX in at its new home at Eglin Air Force Base, Florida. (Photo: US Air Force, Samuel King Jr.)

as something of an 'arsenal plane' for LO fighters, bringing up to 22 air-to-air missiles, 28 Small Diameter Bombs or seven 2,000lb bombs to the fight.

The F-15EX is, to all intents and purposes, a minimum change version of the F-15QA, with

the same life of 20,000 flying hours and the same Open Mission System (OMS) software which promises to enable and facilitate rapid upgrades and capability enhancements.

The US Department of Defense ordered eight F-15EXs in July 2020 (at a cost of $1.2bn),

and the FY2021 defense appropriations bill funded F-15EX procurement at $1.23bn for 12 aircraft. Twelve further aircraft were funded in FY22, with Congress adding an additional five aircraft in FY22. The Fiscal Year 2023 budget request accelerated procurement of the type, but it also included a proposal to decrease the total planned procurement total to just 80 aircraft. Air Force Secretary Frank Kendall reportedly even asked those drawing up the service's budget to consider cancelling the F-15EX altogether! This suggestion was rejected, and the US Air Force's proposed budget for Fiscal Year 2024 included a request for funds for 24 more F-15EX Eagle IIs taking the total planned fleet size up to 104 aircraft, of an originally stated requirement for 144 aircraft. The latest budget documents indicate that the USAF may plan to ask for funds to acquire another 24 F-15EXs in Fiscal Year 2025, bringing the total to 128, and providing for at least one additional Eagle II squadron. This should be enough to re-equip all four remaining ANG F-15C/D squadrons, and the schoolhouse.

The Air National Guard director, Lt Gen Michael Loh, reportedly wants to boost F-15EX numbers. "Some people are still looking at this as a 1970s-technology aircraft. It is not he said. "We have not done a great job of saying, 'Hey, here's how this fits in better, let's say, than an F-15E, and that will be our challenge over the next couple of years. That will then drive different conversations."

The most obvious 'recognition feature' of the F-15EX is provided by the angular ECM antenna fairings on each side of the rear cockpit. They are seen to advantage in this view of EX2 refuelling. (Photo: US Air Force, 2d Lt Mary Begy)

There are good reasons for surging F-15EX procurement to allow it to replace the ageing F-15C/Ds as quickly as possible. Doing so could allow F-35 procurement to be slowed down until the more advanced Block 4 version is ready. And the F-15EX seems to be cheap. Boeing says that it can maintain its $80m unit cost for the F-15EX, despite the effects of inflation and COVID-19, while the aircraft's operating costs are much lower than both older legacy F-15 variants and modern LO aircraft.

The initial $1.2bn contract awarded to Boeing on July 13, 2020 by the US Air Force covered the design, development, integration, manufacturing, test, verification, certification, sustainment, and modification of the F-15EX, including spares, support equipment, training materials and technical support and delivery of the first eight of the 144 planned new build F-15EX fighters.

Maiden flight

The first F-15EX (20-0001, known as EX1) made its maiden flight at St. Louis' Lambert Field on February 2, 2021 in the hands of Boeing's F-15 chief test pilot Matt 'Phat' Giese and fellow test pilot Mike 'Houdini' Quintini. The aircraft was unpainted and was fitted from the start with conformal fuel tanks. The aircraft reached 40,000ft and Mach 2 (the limit with CFTs fitted) during the flight, and even performed some tailslides and other high alpha manoeuvres.

As air defence/air superiority aircraft the USAF F-15EX will not be delivered with CFTs as standard, and the aircraft configuration for the first operational F-15EX units will not include conformal fuel tanks. The first two aircraft were fitted with CFTs during initial Phase 1 testing, however, allowing CFTs to be used operationally

if and when required, and there are plans to procure a limited number of sets of tanks for the F-15EX fleet.

The first production aircraft was delivered to Eglin Air Force Base in Florida on March 11, 2021, where it was tasked with supporting development testing for AFMC. It was marked with 'ET' tail codes signifying its notional assignment to the 96th Test Wing's 40th Flight Test Squadron. It was flown to Eglin by Lt Col Richard Turner, commander of the 40th FLTS, and Lt Col Jacob Lindaman, commander of the 85th TES. On April 8, Eglin Air Force Base served as the location for a formal unveiling of the name and the official role of the F-15EX Eagle ll, in the presence of Lt Gen Duke Richardson, the then principle military deputy for the Office of the Assistant Secretary of the Air Force (Acquisition, Technology and Logistics).

The second aircraft (20-0002) was delivered on April 20, 2021 and was assigned to Air Combat Command for operational testing. EX2 wore 'OT' tail codes representing the 53rd Wing's 85th Test and Evaluation Squadron.

Initial Operational Test and Evaluation of the F-15EX is led by AFOTEC Detachment Six with personnel from Eglin and Nellis Air Force Bases and from the Oregon and Florida National Guard.

Only two months after its arrival at Eglin, the F-15EX deployed to participate in exercise Northern Edge in Alaska. This and other exercises quickly demonstrated that while the platform still needs more development, it is completely capable of fulfilling its expected air dominance role.

The F-15EX is the first new aircraft to be evaluated and fielded via an innovative new rapid acquisition programme that combines developmental and operational test, expediting

the test timeline. It is hoped that this will set a precedent for future aircraft programmes. F-15EXs flew their first operational test sortie from Nellis on October 21, 2021, though the majority of early flight-testing was developmental.

The commander of Air Combat Command, Gen Mark Kelly, flew the F-15EX Eagle II for the first time on September 1, 2021, after completing the requisite academic and simulator training. As a currently qualified F-15E pilot with more than 6,000 hours in multiple aircraft types, Kelly became the second pilot to have flown both the F-15EX and F-35A. This gave him a unique insight into the air force's vision of how these two fighters will integrate in the future.

"When folks talk about fourth and fifth-generation fighters, it's important to zero out the ambiguity of exactly 'what' they are referring to. Are we talking about signature, avionics, sensors/sensor fusion, and weapons? Because there is absolutely zero doubt that fourth-generation aircraft equipped with fifth-generation sensors, avionics, and weapons bring disruptive and decisive effects to a peer fight. This airframe is a part of future force structure changes that are key to creating a fighter fleet that meets air superiority needs for our nation's defence," Kelly said. "As the command in charge of OT&E for the new fighter force structure, ACC will work to develop a fleet that can ensure we have a competitive advantage in a future fight."

The F-15EX Eagle II is already making rapid progress. The 40th Flight Test Squadron undertook a successful AIM-120D missile firing using EX1 on January 25, 2022, during which Maj Benjamin Naumann and Maj Mark Smith downed a BQM-167 aerial target ➤

The cockpit of the F-15EX is dominated by a single large area display, which can be configured and optimised to meet any role. (Photo: Boeing)

Flying locally over the Gulf of Mexico, two F-15EX Eagle II aircraft launched missiles from their new weapon stations, known as Stations 1 and 9, on November 29, 2021. Here an AIM-120D is fired from Station 1. (Photo: US Air Force)

drone over the Gulf of Mexico. They were participating in the 53rd Wing's Combat Archer exercise, an air-to-air weapons system evaluation programme. An F-15EX Eagle II fired an AIM-120 AMRAAM missile from one of the fighter's added weapons stations during a test on November 29, 2022, and another fired an AIM-9X from the same new station. Maj Jeremy Schnurbusch, a pilot attached to the 40th Flight Test Squadron, fired the AIM-9X missile, and Maj Brett Hughes of the Operational Flight Program Combined Test Force fired the AIM-120.

Lt Col Christopher Wee, commander of the test force said: "This event, executed by a top-notch team of test pilots, engineers and experts proves yet again that the F-15EX will be ready if, and when, our adversaries challenge our nation's interests. The F-15EX is an incredible addition to the USAF inventory."

Six further Lot 1 aircraft will be delivered to Eglin AFB in fiscal year 2023, and at least 76 more will follow over the next five years.

As expected, differences between the F-15QA and the USAF's new F-15EX have proved to be relatively trivial, the new USAF Eagles being

US Air Force Lt Col Richard Turner, 40th Flight Test Squadron commander flew the unit's senior enlisted leader, MSgt Tristan McIntire, during a test sortie in the F-15EX Eagle II over the Gulf of Mexico on June 14, 2022. (Photo: US Air Force, Tech Sgt John McRell)

The 53rd Wing welcomed the second F-15EX Eagle II to Eglin Air Force Base, Florida, on April 20, 2021. The 40th Flight Test Squadron and 85th Test and Evaluation Squadron worked together to undertake an integrated developmental and operational testing programme. (Photo: US Air Force, 1st Lt Savanah Bray)

fitted with the Eagle Passive Active Warning Survivability System (EPAWSS) also being integrated on the F-15E, and using the same OFP (Operational Flight Program) Suite 9 software, which dovetails with the current F-15E Strike Eagle and F-15C standard, where the F-15QA uses a bespoke customer Operational Flight Program (OFP) software.

The exact software standard used by the F-15EX originally was Operational Flight Program software Suite 9.1 'X', comparable and near-common with the Suite 9.1 'RR' software currently testing and preparing to field on USAF F-15Cs and F-15Es. FY22 efforts are focusing on integrating F-15EX-unique software into the common F-15 Operational Flight Program.

The original plan was for the 173rd Fighter Wing at Kingsley Field Air National Guard Base, Klamath Falls, Oregon (which currently serves as the F-15C/D training unit) to become the F-15EX Formal Training Unit (FTU) beginning in 2022. The Oregon ANG's other F-15C unit, the 142nd Fighter Wing at Portland, Oregon, was to have become the first operational unit to fly the F-15EX in 2023, with Initial Operational Capability planned for the same year. The Florida Air National Guard was then expected to be the second operator of the F-15EX.

The schedule for the 142nd getting its Eagle IIs subsequently slipped by two years and the plans for the 173rd were thrown into disarray, and other units now seem likely to be the first with the F-15EX.

The Air Force now plans to re-equip the remaining operational Air National Guard F-15C/D bases which will use the new aircraft for critical homeland defence alert missions. The National Guard Bureau examined bed down plans for two F-15EX squadrons (each with 21 aircraft with three back-ups) and one squadron of F-35A aircraft (21 aircraft and two backups).

The F-15EXs were to be stationed at two of three alternative locations - Barnes Air National Guard Base at Westfield-Barnes Regional Airport, Westfield, Massachusetts, Fresno Air National Guard Base at Fresno Yosemite International Airport, Fresno, California and Naval Air Station Joint Reserve Base, New Orleans, Belle Chasse, Louisiana. The same three bases were examined as potential F-35A operating bases, together with Naval Air Station Lemoore, California.

In the end the recommendation was for the F-35A to be based at Barnes Airport, Massachusetts (joining Jacksonville Air National Guard Base, Florida, which will begin receiving F-35 Lightning IIs in 2024). The F-15EXs will go to Fresno Yosemite Airport, and Naval Air Station Joint Reserve Base New Orleans, from 2027-28. There are no plans to equip any active duty squadrons with the F-15EX, so far.

Some believe that the US Air Force may be looking now to consolidate the F-15E and F-15EX training at a single 'schoolhouse' unit, possibly training all F-15E and F-15EX pilots on the F-15E first, with only a quick EX conversion

at the squadron level. That would free up a number of F-15EX aircraft once provisionally earmarked for the FTU to equip an additional operational squadron.

Speculation

There has been speculation that it would be better to replace the ANG F-15Cs with a combination of repurposed F-15Es, upgraded F-16s, F-35As, and perhaps even a homeland defence fighter derivative of the T-7A, using F-15EX to replace the F-15Es and Kadena-based F-15Cs, where they could better support the National Defense Strategy.

The F-15Es would be a marked improvement over current F-15Cs in the homeland defence role, since they have better sensor integration, an integrated Sniper pod, optional conformal fuel tanks, and a fully funded EPAWSS (Eagle Passive Active Warning Survivability System). Procurement of the Advanced Missile and Bomb Ejection Rack (AMBER) rack system would increase air to air missile capacity to 14 missiles.

The head of Pacific Air Forces, Gen Kenneth Wilsbach has already said that he would like to see the Eagle II replacing Kadena's two squadrons of F-15C/Ds. "What we intend to use it for there, if we're so fortunate to get that replacement, is air superiority and some long-range weapons capabilities that you can conduct on the F-15EX," Wilsbach said.

The future may be bright for the F-15EX, but it's not clear what that future is! ∎

Lockheed Martin F-16 Fighting Falcon

Despite its age and limitations (which are being addressed in an ambitious and far-reaching upgrade) the F-16 remains an impressive performer and dominates the USAF's tactical fighter fleet.

The F-16 Fighting Falcon, also known as the Viper, is a lightweight, multi-role fighter that fulfils air-to-air, CAS, SEAD, interdiction, all-weather strike, FAC-A, and tactical nuclear delivery missions. The aircraft's kinematic performance and agility remain extremely competitive, and a lightly loaded F-16 is still an extremely effective aircraft in

WVR combat, though in some other respects the aircraft is showing its age, especially with regard to sensor performance. The fundamental soundness of its basic design makes the aircraft extremely well-suited to modernisation and upgrade, and there have been a number of attempts to produce modernised and improved F-16 variants and derivatives.

Despite having made its first flight almost 50 years ago, the Lockheed Martin F-16 remains in widespread use, and is still the most widely operated fighter in service today. Nearly 3,000 of the 4,588 F-16s put into service since 1978 are still in use with 25 air forces today (an estimated 2,180 single-seat variants and 620 two-seat trainer variants). This represents about

An F-16C Fighting Falcon of the 480th Fighter Squadron, painted in the new 'Have Glass' stealthy paint scheme, departs after receiving fuel from a 50th Expeditionary Aircraft Refueling Squadron KC-135 Stratotanker, during a mission over Southwest Asia, on December 22, 2020. The F-16 provides the backbone of the tactical aircraft fleet. (Photo: US Air Force, Staff Sgt Trevor T. McBride)

An F-16C Falcon assigned to the 64th Aggressor Squadron, taxies out prior to a Red Flag mission at Nellis Air Force Base, on August 4, 2021. Older F-16s provide the backbone of the aggressor fleet. (Photo: US Air Force, William R. Lewis)

15% of the world's operational fighter fleet. The Viper forms about half of the USAF's fighter inventory, with 441 F-16Cs and 108 two-seat F-16Ds in the Active Duty force, 287 F-16Cs and 45 F-16Ds in the Air National Guard, and 52 F-16Cs and a pair of F-16Ds in AFRC. These are what remain of about 2,206 F-16s produced for the USAF and have an average age of 31 years.

The USAF F-16C/D fleet can be further divided into two – the so-called 'Pre-Block' aircraft (230 Blocks 25, 30 and 32 examples) and the 651 'Post Block' (Block 40, 42, 50 and 52) F-16s. The 'Post-Block' F-16s have already been brought to a common standard with updated cockpit displays, new mission computers, and datalinks under the $1 billion Common Configuration Implementation Program (CCIP) which ran from 2000 until 2010. The USAF is currently retiring some of its Pre-Block aircraft (including 47 airframes in FY22), but additional Pre-Block divestment details were deemed sensitive and were omitted from the US Government Accountability Office (GAO) report into tactical aircraft.

The USAF is, however, upgrading and modernising the Post-Block fleet for service into the late 2040s.

There are also 66 QF-16A manned/unmanned aerial target and threat simulator aircraft. The QF-16s began to replace the dwindling and obsolescent fleet of QF-4 Full-Scale Aerial Targets in 2015. Boeing was put under contract to deliver 121 converted airframes in five production lots through April 2021, with 12 further conversions in FY22. The aircraft were converted at Davis-Monthan, Arizona, and Cecil Field in Jacksonville, Florida. In September 2021 there were 17 QF-16As and 49 QF-16Cs in the inventory. The QF-16As were converted from retired F-16A Block 15s, and the QF-16Cs from retired F-16C Block 25s and Block 30s.

Within Air Combat Command the F-16 equips three active duty squadrons of the ▶

Colonel Kristoffer Smith, commander of the 20th Fighter Wing, performs pre-flight checks during exercise Red Flag-Nellis 23-2 on March 20, 2023. The F-16 continues to provide the USAF with its dedicated SEAD/ DEAD capabilities. (Photo: US Air Force, Staff Sgt Madeline Herzog)

A US Air Force F-16 Fighting Falcon assigned to the 77th Expeditionary Fighter Squadron seen flying a mission in the US Central Command Area of responsibility, on March 20, 2023. (Photo: US Air Force, Tech Sgt Daniel Asselta)

20th Fighter Wing at Shaw AFB, and the 53rd Wing (ACC) at Eglin AFB, while the 57th Wing at Nellis AFB in Nevada includes an aggressor squadron, and the Thunderbirds display team.

PACAF includes two F-16 squadrons serving with the 8th Fighter Wing at Kunsan AB in South Korea, two with the 35th Fighter Wing at Misawa AB in Japan, two with the 51st Fighter Wing at Osan AB in South Korea and one aggressor squadron with 354th Fighter Wing at Eielson AFB in Alaska.

USAFE/AFAFRICA includes two F-16 squadrons serving with the 31st Fighter Wing at Aviano AB in Italy and one serves with the 52nd Fighter Wing at Spangdahlem AB in Germany.

Three AFRC squadrons are equipped with the F-16, these being assigned to the 301st Fighter Wing NAS JRB at Fort Worth in Texas, the 482nd Fighter Wing at Homestead ARB in Florida,

and the 944th Fighter Wing at Luke AFB in Arizona.

Within the Air National Guard (ANG) F-16s serve with one squadron of the Alabama ANG's 187th Fighter Wing at Montgomery Regional Airport, two squadrons of the Arizona ANG's 162nd Fighter Wing at Tucson, one squadron of the Colorado Guard's 140th Wing at Buckley Space Force Base, one squadron of the District of Columbia ANG's 113th Wing at Andrews AFB, one squadron of the 148th Fighter Wing (Minnesota ANG) at Duluth International Airport, one squadron of the New Jersey ANG's 177th Fighter Wing at Atlantic City, and one

An F-16C rolls inverted to break away from the tanker while popping IR decoy flares. The aircraft was operating over Iraq on November 9, 2011. The F-16 has served with distinction in US operations in the Middle East, Afghanistan, and the Balkans. (Photo: US Air Force, Master Sgt Cecilio Ricardo)

squadron of the Ohio ANG's 180th Fighter Wing at Toledo. F-16s also equip one squadron of the Oklahoma ANG's 138th Fighter Wing at Tulsa, one squadron of the South Carolina ANG's 169th Fighter Wing at McEntire Joint National Guard Station, one squadron of the 114th Fighter Wing, South Dakota ANG at Joe Foss Field, one squadron of the 149th Fighter Wing, Texas ANG at Kelly Field Annex and one squadron of the 115th Fighter Wing at Truax Field with the Wisconsin ANG, though this is due to convert to the F-35A. Another F-16 squadron is planned to stand up at Fort Wayne Airport, Indiana.

Within AETC the 54th Fighter Group (part of the 49th Wing) at Holloman AFB in New Mexico includes five training units while the 56th Fighter Wing at Luke AFB in Arizona includes four F-16 squadrons. F-16s also serve with the test units at Eglin AFB in Florida and Edwards

The 20th Fighter Wing flagship formed part of a four-ship formation of F-16 Fighting Falcons flying over Shaw Air Force Base, on 21 July, 2017, as part of a commemoration of the hundredth anniversary of the 55th Fighter Squadron. The formation consisted of aircraft from the 55th, 77th, and 79th fighter squadrons all stationed at Shaw AFB. (Photo: US Air Force, Tech Sgt Gregory Brook)

AFB in California, including the 412th Test Wing (AFMC) at Edwards AFB, CA – assigned to Air Force Materiel Command (AFMC).

Development process

The Lightweight Fighter (LWF) competition that spawned the original YF-16 called for a 20,000lb air-to-air day fighter with a good turn rate, acceleration, and range. The aircraft was to be optimised for combat at speeds of Mach 0.6–1.6 and altitudes of 30,000–40,000ft which is where USAF studies predicted most future air combat would occur. The request for proposals was issued on January 6, 1972.

The proponents of the LWF pushed the type as the low cost element in a high-cost/low-cost force mix alongside the F-15. This mix would allow the USAF to afford to procure sufficient fighters to meet its overall fighter force structure requirements.

The prototype YF-16 first flew on February 2, 1974, competing with Northrop's YF-17 in the USAF Lightweight Fighter competition fly-off. In April 1974 US Secretary of Defense James R. Schlesinger announced that the LWF programme was being rolled into a new Air Combat Fighter (ACF) competition, and that the ACF would be a multi-role fighter. The YF-16 had originally been designed as a WVR dogfighter with zero BVR capability, and it was at this point that the aircraft was integrated with BVR Sparrow AAMs and gained air-to-ground capabilities.

On January 13, 1975, Secretary of the Air Force John L. McLucas announced that the YF-16 had been selected as the winner of the ACF competition. The YF-16 design was significantly refined for the production F-16, which was 25% heavier than the prototype, and whereas the original YF-16 was designed as a lightweight

fighter optimised for pure air-to-air combat, the similar looking production F-16 that we know today is a multi-role tactical fighter.

Though the production F-16 is still one of the most manoeuvrable fighters ever built, it is very much a multi-role fighter capable of CAS, SEAD, interdiction, FAC-A, tactical nuclear strike, and all-weather attack as well as air-to-air missions. It is a fighter-bomber that carries the majority of the USAF's in-service PGMs.

This was a remarkable transformation, and even more remarkable was that it was achieved without a radical overhaul of the basic design. The configuration remained much the same, to the extent that few could have confidently told the first production F-16A from the YF-16, just by looking at it.

The new, production F-16A Fighting Falcon used the same basic relaxed static stability/fly-by-wire flight control system as the YF-16, ▶

An F-16 Fighting Falcon from the 55th Expeditionary Fighter Squadron flies alongside a pair of Israeli Air Force F-16s during Exercise Desert Falcon in Israel, on January 16, 2022. Desert Falcon is a joint international exercise in which the Israeli and US aircrews fly various aerial scenarios and strikes. (Photo: Israeli Air Force)

and retained a frameless bubble canopy for good visibility, a side-mounted control stick and an ejection seat that was reclined by 30° for improved *g*-tolerance. The fuselage was lengthened by 10.6in, a larger nose radome was fitted to allow the AN/APG-66 radar to be installed, wing area was increased, the tailfin height was decreased, the ventral fins were enlarged, and two more underwing hardpoints were added.

The first production F-16A made its maiden flight on December 8, 1976 and was followed by the two-seat F-16B on August 8, 1977. Deliveries of production F-16As began in August 1978, and the first operational F-16A was delivered to the 388th Tactical Fighter Wing at Hill Air Force Base, Utah in January 1979 and the USAF declared F-16A initial operating capability in October 1980.

The single seat F-16C and two seat F-16D entered production in 1984, introducing improved avionics and radar and adding beyond-visual-range (BVR) capability using AIM-7 and AIM-120 air-air missiles. F-16C/D deliveries began with Block 25 and the aircraft has been delivered in several block standards since then.

The F-16 made its combat debut in Desert Storm in 1991 and has participated in virtually every major USAF operation since then. The Viper scored its first USAF air-to-air kill during Operation Southern Watch on December 27,

An F-16C of the 85th Test and Evaluation Squadron at Eglin AFB fires an AIM-120 AMRAAM from its wingtip launch rail. The F-16 with AMRAAM and an AESA radar is still a compelling proposition. (Photo: US Air Force)

Two QF-16 Vipers from the 82nd Aerial Targets Squadron Detachment 1, taxi on the flight line at Holloman Air Force Base, New Mexico on February 22, 2023. The 82nd ATRS is responsible for providing QF-16s for customers' system tests that require aerial targets for weapons testing. (Photo: US Air Force, Airman 1st Class Isaiah Pedrazzini)

1992. USAF F-16s have achieved six further kills since then, five of them in the Balkans.

All active duty, Air National Guard and Air Force Reserve units have now converted to the F-16C/D, though some export customers still operate F-16A/Bs. Some aggressor units still fly the F-16C/D Block 25 and many ANG, AFRC units field the Block 30/32.

With a maximum take-off weight of 37,500lb the Block 30 variants achieved IOC in 1981. They were the first F-16s to feature the common engine bay, allowing installation of one of two more powerful alternative engines - the Block 30 being powered by the 25,735lb st General Electric F110-GE-100 turbofan, while the Block 32 used the 23,770lb st Pratt & Whitney F100-PW-220.

The F110 required a larger air intake though this change was not made at first, and early F-16C/D Block 30's had the original, small 'normal shock inlet'. A larger 'big mouth' inlet (known as the modular common air intake duct) was adopted for F110-powered Fighting Falcons from F-16C Block 30D #86-0262 onward. It was not possible to adopt a common air intake, and Block 32 aircraft retained the smaller intake shape.

The F100-PW-220 engine used by Block 32 F-16Cs were slightly less powerful than the F100-PW-200 but proved more reliable and less prone to stagnation stalling.

Both inlet types are specially treated with several coatings of radar absorbing material (RAM), reducing radar cross section.

Block 30/32 introduced the Seek Talk secure voice communication system, a voice message unit, and a crash-survivable flight data recorder, as well as seal-bond fuel tanks. From August 1987, provision was made for the AGM-45 Shrike and AGM-88 HARM anti-radiation missiles.

The Block 30B introduced full level IV multi-target capability for the AIM-120 from the Spring of 1987, with expanded memory ➤

An F-16 Fighting Falcon of the 18th Aggressor Squadron manoeuvres into a refuelling position after an air-combat sortie over Joint Pacific Alaska Range Complex on June 18, 2021 in support of Red Flag-Alaska 21-2. Aggressor F-16s wear a variety of colour schemes, mostly based on those seen on Russian and Chinese fighters. (Photo: US Air Force, Airman 1st Class Mario Calabro)

provided for the Programmable Display Generator and the Data Entry Electronics Unit.

Mini-block D introduced double the number of chaff/flare dispensers and the forward RWR antennas were relocated to the leading edge flap. The new 'beer can' antennas have since been retrofitted onto all previous F-16C/Ds.

The Block 40/42 aircraft, also briefly known as the F-16CG/DG, and sometimes as the 'Night Falcon' (due to its enhanced night/ all-weather capabilities) had an MTOW of 42,300lb, increased g-limits and an expanded flight envelope, and achieved IOC in 1989. LANTIRN navigation and targeting pods were integrated, together with the associated wide angle holographic diffractive optics heads-up display (HUD), though early Block 40/42 aircraft were initially fitted with only the AN/AAQ-13 navigation pod, since the targeting pod was delayed as a result of technical difficulties.

The airframe was strengthened, giving a 9G capability at 28,500lb weight, from 26,900lb. The undercarriage legs were lengthened to give more clearance for the two under fuselage LANTIRN pods and were strengthened to handle the increased weight. Larger wheels and tyres necessitated bulged landing gear doors, and the landing lights were moved to the nose gear doors.

Block 40/42 also introduced digital flight controls (replacing the old analogue system),

the AN/APG-68V(5) radar (with a 100+ hour Mean Time Between Failures) and ALE-47 chaff/flare dispensers. A new positive-pressure breathing system was provided to improve *g*-tolerance for the pilot.

In 1995, 38 F-16C/D Block 40 aircraft of USAFE's 31st Fighter Wing based at Aviano AB, Italy, were equipped with Sure Strike, a package consisting of an Improved Data Modem (IDM) and Night Vision Goggles (NVG), giving the aircraft a quick reaction CAS capability for missions over Bosnia. The IDM allowed the aircraft to receive latitude, longitude, and elevation of a target from a FAC (Forward Air Controller) directly into the weapon system computer and then displaying it as a waypoint on the HUD.

In July 1997, Lockheed Martin was awarded a contract to upgrade the Sure Strike system under project Gold Strike. This added two-way imagery transmission to Sure Strike, allowing the pilot to receive video imagery, and to transmit LANTIRN video images from the cockpit.

The Block 50/52 (also known as the F-16CJ) introduced enhanced defence suppression capabilities, with provision for an AN/ASQ-213 HARM targeting pod, a longer-range radar, and even higher thrust 'Improved Performance Engines', which allowed an increase in MTOW

to 48,000lb. The Block 50 used the 29,000lb F110-GE-129 turbofan, while the Block 52 used the similarly rated F100-PW-229. The first Block 50/52 F-16 rolled out at Fort Worth on October 31, 1991 The Block 50/52 achieved IOC in 1994.

Early examples of the Block 50/52 used the Westinghouse AN/APG-68 V(5) radar, while later batches used the V(7) and V(8), versions of the radar, which offered improved performance against air targets.

The standard avionics fit for the Block 50 included a Honeywell H-423 Ring Laser Gyro Inertial Navigation System (RLG INS), a larger capacity Data Transfer Cartridge, IDM, AN/ALR-56M advanced RWR, AN/ALE-47 threat adaptive countermeasure system, an advanced IFF interrogator, and a MIL-STD-1760 databus for programming new-generation PGMs, including JDAM, the AGM-154A/B JSOW and the AGM-84 Harpoon anti-ship missile.

Deliveries of the Block 50D/52D began in May 1993. All but the earliest Block 50 models have been upgraded to the Block 50D standard.

The Block 50D/52D had the HARM Avionics/ Launcher Interface Computer (ALIC), allowing full autonomous HARM missile employment capability, in combination with the AN/ASQ-213 HTS pod mounted on the starboard intake hardpoint. This contains a super-sensitive receiver that detects, classifies, and ranges threats and passes the information to the HARM missile and to the cockpit displays. If the HTS pod is not carried, assets like the RC-135 Rivet Joint aircraft can sort and prioritise targets for the F-16 in dense threat environments.

In the 1980s there were a number of attempts to produce a more advanced F-16 variant, but these foundered. The so-called F-16 Agile Falcon design was proposed as a low-cost alternative in the Advanced Tactical Fighter (ATF) competition in 1984. This had a 25% larger wing, an uprated engine, and some of the MSIP IV improvements that were then being developed for the basic F-16. The Agile Falcon lost out to the F-22, but some of its capabilities were incorporated into the F-16C/D Block 40, and the Agile Falcon's big wing also influenced Japan's Mitsubishi F-2 fighter.

At broadly the same time, the even more radically redesigned, cranked Delta wing, tailless F-16XL was offered for the Enhanced Tactical Fighter (ETF) programme, losing out to the F-15E Strike Eagle in February 1984. The similar F-16X Falcon 2000, proposed in 1993, featured a delta wing based on that of the F-22, and spawned the F-16U offered to the UAE, which also failed to come to fruition.

It became apparent that radical airframe redesign was not going to be cost-effective, and attention switched to more modest upgrade configurations which tended to retain the same basic 'outer mould line' as the basic F-16C/D but incorporating new sensors and systems.

Desert Falcon

The F-16ES (Enhanced Strategic) was an extended-range variant of the F-16C/D intended to be fitted with a low drag internal targeting system based on LANTIRN. The aircraft also

An F-16 Fighting Falcon assigned to the 64th Aggressor Squadron, Nellis Air Force Base, Nevada, takes off in support of Black Flag 22-2, at Nellis Air Force Base, on September 20 2022. (Photo: US Air Force, William R. Lewis)

had provision for conformal fuel tanks that conferred a 40% improvement in range compared to the standard Block 50. The F-16ES was offered to Israel as an alternative to the F-15I Strike Eagle in late 1993, and though it remained stillborn, it did influence the development of the Block 60 F-16E/F for the United Arab Emirates.

The Block 60 F-16E/F Desert Falcon was the most advanced and most capable F-16 ever fielded when it entered service in 2005, with its advanced liquid cooled AN/APG-80 AESA radar, a new EW system, more powerful

General Electric F110-GE-132 engine and internal targeting FLIR, as well as a massive improvement in computing power. Some maintain that it retains that status even to this day, even compared to the latest Block 70 aircraft. *Flight International* observed that this was "the first time that the US has sold a better [F-16] aircraft overseas than its own forces fly."

The Block 60 F-16E/F for the UAE demonstrated what the F-16 could be, but development of this variant had been paid for by the Emiratis and it was not available to other operators. Nor was Japan's Mitsubishi F-2 – an ▶

Preparing to launch an F-16 Fighting Falcon with a new 'ghost' paint scheme applied by the 576th Aircraft Maintenance Squadron at Hill Air Force Base, Utah, on June 3, 2020. The aircraft was test flown by the 514th Flight Test Squadron before being delivered to the 64th Aggressor Squadron at Nellis Air Force Base, Nevada. (Photo: US Air Force, R. Nial Bradshaw)

An F-16C Fighting Falcon, from the 555th Fighter Squadron (also known as 'Triple Nickel') based at Aviano Air Base, Italy, moves away after receiving fuel from a KC-135 Stratotanker, assigned to the 340th Expeditionary Air Refueling Squadron, during a mission over Afghanistan in support of Operation Enduring Freedom, on March 29, 2011. (Photo: US Air Force, Master Sgt William Greer)

F-16 based design with an indigenous Japanese AESA radar. Although these two aircraft proved revelatory in service, the UAE was destined to remain the only customer for the Block 60, and the F-2 remained a JASDF-only aircraft, and it was some time before another AESA-equipped F-16 variant emerged.

There were real fears that an export Block 60 could cannibalise sales of the new F-35

Joint Strike Fighter, but changes to US export regulations quickly rendered many of the F-16E/F's systems unexportable anyway. This derailed a Lockheed Martin bid to offer the F-16 Block 60 to Singapore, while bids to offer similar aircraft to India (the Block 60-based F-16IN), and to Brazil (the so-called Block 62+ F-16BR Super Viper) came to nothing. The aircraft offered to India for the Medium

Multi-Role Combat Aircraft competition and showcased at the 2009 Aero India Air Show was known as the Block 70/72 F-16IN Super Viper, but this unbuilt variant bore no real resemblance to today's Block 70.

Remarkably, even the UAE was unable to receive 30 extra new-build Block 61 F-16E/Fs when it requested them in 2014, and this effectively ended efforts to market versions based on the Desert Falcon.

The USAF's determination to move to an 'all-stealth' combat aircraft fleet killed any chance of selling the Block 60 to the US Air Force, and when the last of 2,231 F-16 fighters for the US Air Force was delivered in March 2005 it was a Block 52 aircraft.

It was widely expected that the Block 50/52 F-16 would be the final USAF F-16, and that the type would quickly be replaced by the stealthy Lockheed Martin F-35A. But delays to the F-35A Joint Strike Fighter programme prevented it from simply and directly replacing the F-16 according to the originally-planned timescale, and this forced the USAF to launch a programme to keep some 300-400 of its Fighting Falcons in service for much longer than had been originally intended, if the USAF was to maintain its force structure, augmenting the slow-growing F-35 force. Under its new plans, the USAF would operate some of its fleet of Block 40-52 F-16 aircraft out to 2048 and beyond.

The F-16 fleet is now cockpit-standardised across all still-active variants with colour MFDs, a modular mission computer, Helmet Mounted Integrated Targeting (HMIT), and Link 16. The Operational Flight Program (OFP) continuously updates the F-16's software across the fleet and

An F-16C Fighting Falcon assigned to the 64th Aggressor Squadron during a Red Flag-Nellis 23-2 mission over the Nevada Test and Training Range, Nevada, on March 23, 2023. The 64th AGRS played as the Red Force during this, one of the US Air Force's largest combat training exercises. (Photo: US Air Force, Senior Airman Zachary Rufus)

most recently added JASSM-ER and enhanced AMRAAM. Ongoing mods include anti-jam UHF communications, MIDS/JTRS for higher capacity, jam-resistant Link 16, Mode 5 IFF, navigation improvements, and an Auto Ground Collision Avoidance System (AGCAS) to prevent flight into terrain. Most of the air force's F-16s will eventually wear the new LO 'Have Glass' paint scheme, using a radar-absorbing coating to replace the Viper's two-tone grey colour scheme.

But it rapidly became clear that a new and more ambitious F-16 upgrade would be required. The upgraded aircraft would be drawn from the USAF's fleet of about 640 Post-Block (Block 40, 42, 50 and 52 F-16Cs and F-16Ds) aircraft, and would equip active-duty, Guard and Reserve squadrons. This upgrade required a twin-track approach, with a structural SLEP (service life extension programme), and with a CAPES (combat avionics programmed extension suite) upgrade to keep the aircraft operationally viable. This would add new capabilities, including data link enhancements and an improved defensive suite, and was intended to enhance combat effectiveness and survivability.

The F-16 SLEP was intended to extend the F-16's airframe life from 8,000 hours to 12,000 hours, thereby adding 8-10 years of extra service life to each airframe, with some aircraft expected to receive replacement wings (or perhaps just upper wing skins and associated fittings), with much of the aircraft's external skin being replaced, together with some airframe structure.

The planned CAPES upgrade was to have seen the integration of a new AESA radar, a new Terma AN/ALQ-213 electronic warfare system, an integrated broadcast system (IBS) and a centre display unit (CDU), together with new operational flight programme software.

The IBS promised a new degree of data fusion, correlating information from the aircraft's own sensors and off-board data from datalinks and presenting these in a single coherent display, with the new CDU providing a high-resolution screen for the IBS, synthetic aperture radar maps and video from targeting pods.

Aerospace Propulsion System specialists assigned to the 148th Fighter Wing, Minnesota Air National Guard, manoeuvre a 3000E trailer under the F110-129 turbofan aircraft engine on an F-16CM Fighting Falcon, on February 28, 2023. The trailer is used to assist with installation and removal of the engine from the F-16.
(Photo: US Air National Guard, Airman 1st Class Tylin Rust)

The automated AN/ALQ-213 electronic warfare suite promised to reduce the pilots' work load, providing a greatly improved man-machine interface.

AESA

But it was the proposed Integration of an Active Electronically Scanned Array – or Antenna (AESA) radar that lay at the heart of the CAPES upgrade, and that was the highest priority. This should come as no surprise, as AESA will almost always represent a major boost in capability compared to an M-scan radar and can offer a generational improvement in capability.

AESA promised to deliver significant improvements in performance – especially in terms of being able to detect targets at longer range but also in terms of track accuracy, which impacts on long range missile effectiveness and kill probability. An Active Electronically

Scanned Array Radar will provide a greater capability to detect, track, and identify low-observable, low-flying, and slow-flying targets. Advanced AESAs like SABR can also be used for non-co-operative target recognition (NCTR), identifying and categorising targets based on their radar signature alone, matching a radar return signature to a specific type of aircraft by its shape and even down to the number of fan blades on target's engine. AESA radars are able to do this with much higher fidelity. AESA also permits synthetic aperture

A US Air Force F-16C Fighting Falcon assigned to the 36th Fighter Squadron (the 'Flying Fiends'), participates in close air support training over Gyeonggi-do, South Korea, on December 20, 2022. The 36th is one of two F-16 squadrons assigned to the 51st Fighter Wing at Osan Air Base, Korea.
(Photo: US Air Force, Staff Sgt. Skyler Combs)

radar mapping for target nomination and engagement.

In the medium term, AESA also offers great potential as a secure datalink, and for electronic attack and non-kinetic effect. Because an AESA radar has no moving parts it also promises a step change in reliability, while the fact that up to about 20% of the transmitter/receiver elements can fail without significantly affecting performance meant that production radars could last for the full lifetime of the aircraft (or even twice the lifetime) without repairs and perhaps even without major maintenance. The F-16 radar retrofit package was designed to fit within the available space, using the same radome, with no 'group-A' structural or wiring modifications required to the aircraft. The upgraded radar therefore included its own liquid-cooling heat exchanger.

Northrop-Grumman had been the radar supplier for all previous production F-16s, supplying both the mechanically-scanned AN/APG-68 radar of the F-16C/D, and the AN/APG-80 active electronically scanned array (AESA) radar used by the Block 60 F-16E/F aircraft.

For CAPES, Northrop-Grumman offered the AN/APG-83 AESA radar, also known as the Scalable Agile Beam Radar (SABR). The AN/APG-83 was developed from the F-35's AN/APG-81 and was always intended as a drop-in AESA replacement for existing F-16 radars.

But Raytheon offered an alternative in the shape of the Raytheon Next Generation Radar or AN/APG-84 (now known as RACR or Raytheon Advanced Combat Radar). This is a scaled-down version of the Super Hornet's AN/APG-79 AESA, using much of the same architecture and active technologies, and the modernised F-15E Strike Eagle's AN/APG-82.

CAPES was cancelled on cost grounds in 2014, as part of the Fiscal Year 2015 budget, but before the project was cancelled, Lockheed Martin selected the Northrop Grumman AN/APG-83 SABR AESA radar over the APG-84 Raytheon Advanced Combat Radar (RACR) for the CAPES upgrade. The same radar was also selected as the basis of its F-16 upgrade for Taiwan, which became the F-16V.

But the requirement for an AESA had not gone away, and in March 2015, the Air Force Life Cycle Management Center (AFLCMC) released a 'sources sought' notice to contractors for a development/production effort to replace the M-scan APG-68 radars of some F-16C/D Block 30-52 aircraft with a new AESA radar – particularly the Air National Guard (ANG) F-16s flying the Aerospace Control Alert mission, and those scheduled to replace ANG F-15C/Ds. F-16Ds from Edwards AFB were used as testbeds for the F-16 Radar Modernization Program (RMP) flying with both SABR and RACR.

In June 2017, the US Air Force selected the AN/APG-83 for an urgent radar upgrade for 72 US Air National Guard F-16s stationed at nine ANG bases throughout the USA. The upgrade was launched to meet a US Northern Command Joint Emergent Operational Need for the homeland defence role, and the ability to counter stealthy cruise missile threats against the homeland was the primary justification for the upgrade.

This upgrade would see these aircraft being upgraded to virtually the same standard as the export F-16V/Block 72. Eventually, the US Air Force hopes to upgrade 372 F-16 aircraft with the AN/APG-83 radar.

The first SABR installation for a front-line USAF F-16 unit was completed in January 2020, on a Block 30 F-16C of the 113th Wing, District of Columbia ANG at Joint Base Andrews, Maryland. Other units equipped included the Oklahoma Air National Guard at Tulsa, the South Dakota Air National Guard at Joe Foss Field, Sioux Falls, and the Minnesota Air National Guard at Duluth Air National Guard Base.

In the process, it was found that it took only a day and a half to swap in a new AN/APG-83 on an F-16.

The USAF launched a remarkably similar upgrade effort in 2015 as the Radar Modernization Program (RMP), aiming to develop a full APG-83 capability for up to 330 active component

F-16s. Some 450 Post-Block airframes were by then undergoing a SLEP which will extend their airframe lives beyond 8,000 flying hours, and 330 of these were also scheduled to receive a digital RWR (as part of a future, fully integrated EW suite), as well as mission computer and cockpit display upgrades. There were other improvements too, including software upgrades to allow the integration of new precision weapons and enhanced avionics. The number had originally been increased from 330 to 450, and then to 512 and finally to 608 Post-Block aircraft.

This $6.3bn upgrade is known as the Post Block Integration Team, or PoBIT programme,

A US Air Force F-16CM Fighting Falcon from the 480th Fighter Squadron flies over Germany on April 13, 2022, after completing installation of a new AN/APG-83 active electronically scanned array (AESA) radar system. This photo was censored for security purposes by blurring out the aircraft's serial number. (Photo: US Air Force, Staff Sgt Chanceler Nardone)

which also includes "up to 22 modifications designed to improve lethality and ensure the fourth-generation fighter remains effective in meeting current and future threats." PoBIT will bring these 608 aircraft to virtual Block 70 standards.

The 480th Fighter Squadron 'Warhawks' at Spangdahlem Air Base became the first active-duty USAF F-16 fighter squadron to receive the AN/APG-83 SABR AESA radar upgrade, from early 2022. Though a press release and official photo were issued, the latter was censored, the aircraft's serial number being obscured.

The 35th Fighter Wing at Misawa was the second USAF unit to receive AESA-upgraded aircraft. Lt Col Josh Plocinski, of the 13th Fighter Squadron fighter pilot, made the first flight in an F-16 Fighting Falcon (92-0912) fitted with a new active electronically scanned array (AESA) radar upgrade on December 5, 2022.

A similarly upgraded Fighting Falcon re-joined the 8th Fighter Wing's Wolf Pack at Osan, South Korea, on April 4, 2023, flown by Colonel John D. Caldwell, 8th FW vice commander. "The upgraded equipment I flew with today greatly improved my situational awareness, allowing me to receive and process information at a much faster rate than other F-16s in the past," Caldwell said. "The information was quick, reliable, and presented on the new displays in a way that reduced my workload and improved effectiveness for all aspects of the flight.

"The F-16 is planned to continue service into the 2040's, so this upgrade is critical to making sure we are keeping pace with the evolving threat environment. The main components that I interacted with today - the CDU and APG-83 SABR - are both critical pieces that work together to bring the F-16 closer to fifth-generation capabilities, which will keep the F-16 relevant to the fight."

Capt Michael C. Durham, the 8th Operations Support Squadron's Weapons Tactics Officer explained that: "The upgraded radar, specifically, allows us to track a greater number of targets at longer ranges in both cooperative

US Air Force Airman 1st Class Kylie Robey, of the 52nd Aircraft Maintenance Squadron, works to install a new active electronically scanned array (AESA) radar system onto a 480th Fighter Squadron F-16C Fighting Falcon at Spangdahlem Air Base, Germany, on May 20, 2022. (Photo: US Air Force, Tech Sgt Maeson L. Elleman)

and non-permissive environments while also improving the F-16's all-weather capabilities by adding synthetic aperture radar mapping for target nomination and engagement."

Caldwell pointed out that: "With regards to the Wolf Pack's 'Take the Fight North' mission, these upgrades primarily allow us to keep pace with near-peer threats, but also have a large hand in the deterrence mission. It will definitely be a part of the decision calculus for the Democratic People's Republic of Korea (DPRK), because the more lethal and survivable we can make our forces here on the peninsula, the more likely we are to deter aggression. The goal is to present a force so capable, that the DPRK decides, instead of pulling a trigger, to pick up the phone to talk. Of course, if deterrence breaks down, the modernisation programme will significantly

improve our ability to defend South Korea and take the fight north if necessary."

With just 72 aircraft retrofitted with AN/APG-83, the Air National Guard's F-16 squadrons will not be able to deploy many AESA equipped aircraft simultaneously. To compensate for this, the Guard will deploy Northrop-Grumman AN/ASQ-236 radar pods on its F-16s.

The AN/ASQ-236 pod is an externally mounted Active Electronically Scanned Array (AESA) pod that provides detailed maps for surveillance, coordinate generation and bomb impact assessment. The pod enables combat air forces to geo-locate points of interest day or night in adverse weather. The pod is already operational on the F-15E Strike Eagle.

The 148th Fighter Wing, which flies the Block 50 F-16CM, has been designated as the ▶

An F-16 Fighting Falcon assigned to the 8th Fighter Wing, Kunsan Air Base, Republic of Korea, flies over the Korean Peninsula, on April 4, 2023 in the hands of Col. John D. Caldwell, 8 FW vice commander. The aircraft had just returned to Kunsan after receiving Post Block Integration Team (PoBIT) upgrades, including installation of the SABR AESA radar. (Photo: US Air Force, Captain Kaylin P. Hankerson)

Lt Col Benjamin Wysack, Lt Col Stephen Graham, Jack Harman, and Maj Justing Eagan flew the first-ever formation of F-16 Fighting Falcons equipped with Active Electronically Scanned Array (AESA) radars from Eglin Air Force Base, on July 2, 2020. The mission included F-16s and F-15s flown by civilian, contractor, Reservist, Guard, and Active Duty pilots who conducted combined developmental and operational testing.
(Photo: US Air Force, Jack Harman)

Air National Guard's centre of excellence for the AN/ASQ-236, and in January 2023 exercised end-to-end employment of the recently fielded AN/ASQ-236 radar pod, in conjunction with subject matter experts from Air Combat Command, Air Force Materiel Command, the Air National Guard, Air Force Life Cycle Management Center, and the Air Force Reserve Test Center.

USAF planning documents revealed in 2021 indicated that the air force was looking at an F-16 successor, which the USAF dubbed as the 'MR-F' or 'MR-X'. USAF Chief of Staff General Charles Q. Brown Jr. said that this future multirole fighter would be a "clean sheet design," which he referred to as a "fourth-and-a half/fifth-gen minus" aircraft, for service from the mid-2030s. He envisaged an aircraft with a fully open architecture to allow rapid capability upgrades. "While I don't have any firm requirement for an F-16 replacement, I know the MR-F piece is going to continue to be looked at, because at some point we'll have to have a replacement for the F-16," Brown averred.

The new fighter was intended to keep hours and wear and tear off the USAF's high end fighters, "I want to moderate how much we're using those aircraft. You don't drive your Ferrari to work every day, you only drive it on Sundays. This is our 'high end' fighter, we want to make sure we don't use it all for the low-end fight," Brown explained.

Assistant Secretary of the Air Force for Acquisition, Technology, and Logistics Will Roper said that the F-35A was "a long way from being an affordable fighter that we can buy in bulk." He added that he expected to see other trade-offs in F-35 numbers and capability mixes with other aircraft types. In an interview with *Aviation Week*'s Steve Trimble, Roper also revealed that the air force was looking at new F-16 purchases. "As you look at the new F-16 production line in South Carolina, that system has some wonderful, upgraded capabilities that are worth thinking about as part of our capacity solution," he said.

But Charles Q. Brown has said that he does not expect to place an order for an advanced F-16 variant like the latest Block 70/72 version. The F-16's future in the USAF therefore remains unclear. ∎

US Air Force pilots finish a pre-flight briefing before testing the new APG-83 Active Electronically Scanned Array radar at Eglin Air Force Base, on July 2, 2020.
(Photo: US Air Force, Master Sgt Tristan McIntire)

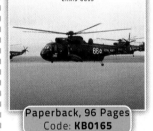

Lockheed Martin F-35A Lightning II Joint Strike Fighter

The F-35A is the most controversial fighter in the USAF's inventory. Slated by many on the grounds of cost, technical problems and poor availability, the Lightning II is viewed by others as being the most advanced and most capable tactical fighter in service anywhere. Both sides are right!

The F-35A is a product of the most expensive weapons acquisition programme in history, has been subject to scandalous mismanagement and has suffered severe technical problems that have resulted in delay and cost. The F-35A remains late and over-budget. In service, it suffers from poor availability and imposes heavy demands on maintenance personnel, while suffering from very high operating and sustainment costs. And many of these problems remain unsolved today, and some are officially classed as having a 'critical impact on mission readiness'.

But the F-35A is also probably the most advanced and most capable tactical fighter in service anywhere. The fact that the term 'fifth-generation' had to be redefined to allow the F-35 to qualify (dropping inconveniences like supercruise performance and super manoeuvrability) is largely a historical irrelevance, as few today even remember Lockheed Martin's original definition – drawn up as a marketing gimmick when the F-22 was born.

The F-35A is a versatile, stealthy, multi-role, penetrating, all-weather fighter/attack aircraft that has the power to "dominate the skies – anytime, anywhere," and that also has an unmatched ability to survive in the advanced threat environment in which it was designed to operate. The F-35A, in short, gives its pilots the critical advantage against any adversary, enabling them to successfully execute their mission and come home safe.

The configuration of the F-35 echoed that of the F-22, with an 'edge-aligned' trapezoidal wing and tailplanes and canted vertical fins. The same basic configuration has been repeated in a number of subsequent LO fighters – including the KAI KF-21, TAI's new MMU, and China's J-31/35 - such that it now seems to be emblematic of the fifth-generation. The aircraft has particularly noteworthy over-the-nose visibility.

In air combat, the F-35A will always get 'first look', thanks to its own miniscule signature and its unprecedented situational awareness. This is, in part, down to the capability offered by its own onboard sensors, but also by its ability to exploit offboard sensors. When those onboard sensors include the Northrop Grumman AN/APG-81 active electronically scanned array (AESA) radar, the Northrop Grumman/Raytheon AN/AAQ-37 Distributed

OT tail codes identify this F-35A Lightning II as an aircraft assigned to operational test duties with the 422nd Test and Evaluation Squadron, at Nellis Air Force Base, Nevada. The aircraft is seen here taking off for a Weapons School Integration mission at Nellis Air Force Base, Nevada, on November 21, 2022. (Photo: US Air Force, William R. Lewis)

Aperture System (DAS), and the multi-aperture Lockheed Martin AN/AAQ-40 Electro-Optical Targeting System (EOTS) unmatched situational awareness is all but guaranteed. The F-35A's advanced sensor package gathers, fuses, and distributes more information than any fighter in history, providing its operators with a decisive information advantage.

The F-35A is equipped with a Northrop Grumman AN/APG-81 active electronically scanned array (AESA) fire control radar, claimed by its manufacturer to be "the latest and most capable AESA in the world," providing "unparalleled battlespace situational awareness that translates into lethality, aircrew effectiveness and survivability." This was almost certainly true in 2005, when the company made the first test flights with the radar, but it may no longer be the case, with new AESA radars in service with advanced repositioners giving a much larger field of regard.

That the APG-81 may no longer enjoy the lead it once did may be gauged by the fact that a new radar, the AN/APG-85, is now under development for the Block 4 F-35A.

The existing AN/APG-81 radar will continue to provide the cornerstone of the F-35's advanced sensor suite until the Block 4 aircraft enters service, and for earlier F-35 aircraft beyond then. The radar incorporates long-range active and passive air-to-air and air-to-ground modes that support a full range of air-to-air and air-to-surface missions along with significant electronic warfare and intelligence, surveillance, and reconnaissance functions.

US Air Force Capt Brad Matherne, a 422nd Test and Evaluation Squadron pilot, models the new helmet used by F-35A pilots. When photographed he was about to fly a training mission on April 4, 2013, at Nellis Air Force Base. (Photo: US Air Force, Senior Airman Brett Clashman)

The AESA's multi-function array (MFA) can operate as an EW aperture for electronic protection (EP), electronic attack (EA) and electronic support measures (ESM), giving the F-35 the ability to defeat enemy jammers, and to suppress the most advanced enemy air defences.

Since the AN/APG-81 was selected for the Joint Strike Fighter in 2001, Northrop Grumman has produced and delivered more than 1,000 APG-81 radars in 11 production lots over two decades. And the company has reduced production costs by more than 70%.

An F-35 Lightning II seen during a combat power exercise at Hill Air Force Base on November 19, 2018. The exercise aimed to confirm the base's ability to quickly employ a larger force of aircraft against air and ground targets and demonstrate the readiness and lethality of the F-35A. The 388th and 419th Fighter Wings were the first combat-ready F-35 units in the air force, ready to deploy anywhere in the world at a moment's notice. (Photo: US Air Force, A1C James Kennedy)

A line up of test jets (AF-1, AF-2, AF-3, AF-4, AF-6, and AF-7) at Edwards AFB, California in May 2011. The line-up is headed by the first production aircraft AF-01, wearing colourful markings. (Photo: Lockheed Martin)

The F-35's other sensors include the Northrop Grumman AN/AAQ-37 DAS, an Electro-Optical Distributed Aperture System (DAS). This system provides pilots with situational awareness in a sphere around the aircraft for enhanced missile warning, aircraft warning, and day/night pilot vision. A new system supplied by Raytheon will replace the existing DAS on aircraft from Lot 15 onwards. The new system promises to deliver over $3bn in life cycle cost savings, a 45% reduction in unit recurring costs, more than 50% reduction in operating and sustainment costs, five times greater reliability, and twice the performance capability.

EOTS

The aircraft is also equipped with an Electro-Optical Targeting System, which combines forward-looking infrared and infrared search and track functionality. The internally mounted EOTS is analogous, in some ways, to a repackaged Litening or Sniper targeting pod, carried internally. The system provides extended range detection and precision targeting against ground targets, plus long range detection of air-to-air threats, enhancing the F-35 pilots' situational awareness and allowing him or her to identify areas of interest, perform reconnaissance and precisely and accurately deliver laser and GPS-guided weapons. From Block 4, the F-35A will use the new Advanced EOTS system, an evolutionary development designed to

The AN/APG-81 AESA's solid-state technology has allowed the elimination of mechanical moving parts while the use of replaceable sub-assemblies has dramatically improved product reliability. The design of the radar has enabled faster and easier repairs to hardware and software modules resulting in significantly lower lifecycle costs when compared to legacy systems. The AN/APG-81 active array has almost twice the expected life of the airframe while at the same time providing the operator with outstanding operational readiness – stated to be greater than 99%, with flight line repair times of less than 30 minutes.

Maj Jonathan 'Spades' Gilbert, taxies out at an icy Eielson AFB, Alaska, in AF-02 on 8 November, 2017. (Photo: US Air Force)

F-35A Lightning II aircraft receive fuel from a KC-10 Extender from Travis Air Force Base, during a flight from England to the US on July 13, 2015, after participating in the world's largest air show, the Royal International Air Tattoo. Early F-35As had very distinctive panel lines, with a different coloured coating around their edges. (Photo: US Air Force, SSgt Madelyn Brown)

replace the original EOTS. Advanced EOTS incorporates a wide range of enhancements and upgrades, including short-wave infrared, high-definition television, an infrared marker, and improved image detector resolution. These enhancements increase recognition and detection ranges, enabling greater overall targeting performance.

The EOTS cameras feed imagery to the F-35's helmet mounted display system, which is claimed to be the most advanced system of its kind. The pilots are able to view mission-critical information in their visor, focused at infinity so that they don't have to refocus their eyes. The way in which the helmet is linked to the EOTS cameras means that the pilot has an unobstructed 360° view of the F-35's external environment – allowing the pilot to effectively 'see through' his own aircraft, without needing to turn or bank.

All of the intelligence and targeting information that an F-35 pilot needs to complete the mission is displayed on the helmet's visor, giving him or her enhanced situational awareness of the battlespace.

The F-35 contains state-of-the-art tactical data links that provide for the secure sharing of data between flight elements. The secure Multifunction Advanced Datalink (MADL) allows F-35As to share their sensor picture, and other forms of data. But it is more difficult for the F-35 to communicate with other assets while preserving its low observability.

F-35s can send information to other aircraft via Link 16, which uses a widely adopted waveform.

But doing so would increase the likelihood of an enemy being able to locate and track an F-35 via those emissions, which are omni-directional and not very LPI/LPD (low probability of interception/detection) in nature.

F-35As can connect with F-22 Raptors while preserving their 'stealth mode'. The Freedom 550 software-programmable radio allows two-way communication between F-35As and F-22s (which have their own Intra-Flight Data Link (IFDL) using a different, incompatible wave form), sending Internet Protocol (IP) packets of data through tailored waveforms to transmit combat-relevant information. The same system was used in the RAF's 2017 two-week BABELFISH III trial, to allow communications between the F-35 and the Typhoon by translating MADL messages to Link 16 format. BABELFISH, built on the USAF's Jetpack 5th to 4th JCTD (Joint Capability Technology Demonstration) in 2014, when Northrop Grumman demonstrated a 'fifth-to-fourth' generation networking capability.

Additionally, in 2020, the USAF demonstrated the use of a new Open Systems Gateway, known as the 'Hydra payload', carried by a U-2S, acting as a 'translator' between the F-35A and F-22 data links. The core of the Hydra OSG is an Open Mission Systems (OMS) compliant Enterprise Mission Computer 2 (EMC2), colloquially known as the 'Einstein Box', an advanced open-architecture mission computer designed to rapidly integrate new and improved functionality.

This kind of datalink expands the range of missions that F-35s can undertake and enables the real-time sharing of some targeting data between the F-35 and other aircraft, and with surface and ground-based platforms, though this remains limited.

Its sensor capabilities make the F-35 much more than a fighter. By operating its advanced sensors and communications suite close to the battlefield and from an elevated position the F-35 is a powerful ISR platform in its own right, while also serving as a force multiplier that can significantly enhance the capabilities of networked airborne, maritime, space, surface, and ground-based platforms.

And while the F-35 may not have quite the agility and turn performance of a clean F-16, nor the sheer 'grunt' of a Typhoon, it is no slouch, with 9g capability, and enjoying a superb instantaneous turn performance and plenty of power. And in any case, the F-35's formidable 360° situational awareness and off boresight capabilities make a traditional dogfight unlikely.

In a BVR engagement, the F-35's tiny radar cross section and formidable situational awareness compensate for any marginal disadvantage in supersonic acceleration. The F-35's relatively modest loadout of BVR missiles is more of a disadvantage, along with the aircraft's continued reliance on the AIM-120 AMRAAM, though the new AIM-260 should soon be integrated, along with the superb MBDA Meteor, though the USAF has no plans to acquire the latter for its F-35s.   ➤

In the air-to-ground role, the F-35A is if anything, even more impressive.

The F-35A's next-generation stealth and advanced avionics and systems are a battle-winning combination. Impressive processing power, open architecture, sophisticated sensors, information fusion and flexible communication links combine to give enhanced situational awareness while LO 'stealth' provides enhanced survivability in even the most contested threat environments. This allows the F-35 to venture where no other aircraft can, negating adversaries' A2/AD (Anti Access/Area Denial) strategies.

Small wonder that its supporters claim that the F-35A is the most lethal, survivable, and connected fighter jet in the world. Connectivity is vital for F-35 sustainment, as well as for operations.

ALIS

The F-35 was the first tactical aircraft system to have sustainment tools designed in concert with the air vehicle to optimise operations. The original ALIS (Autonomic Logistics Information System) served as the information infrastructure for F-35A logistics and support, forming a single, secure information environment that provided users with up-to-date aircraft health and maintenance information - using web-enabled applications on a distributed network.

An F-35A Lightning II of the 388th Fighter Wing at Hill AFB, Utah, flies over the US Central Command area of responsibility, on July 17, 2020. For 'Day 1' missions. The F-35A carries only internal weapons, to minimise the aircraft's radar cross section. (Photo: US Air Force, A1C Duncan C. Bevan)

ALIS integrated current performance data, operational parameters, current configuration, scheduled upgrades and maintenance, component history, predictive diagnostics (prognostics) and health management, as well as operations scheduling, training, mission planning and service support for the F-35. It was supposed to perform behind-the-scenes monitoring, maintenance, and prognostics to support the aircraft and ensure continued availability, while enhancing operational planning and execution.

ALIS worked by receiving health reporting codes while the F-35 was still in flight, using a radio frequency downlink. It then transmitted aircraft health and maintenance action information to the appropriate users on a globally-distributed network that could be accessed by technicians worldwide. The system enabled the pre-positioning of parts and any specialised maintainers on the ground when the aircraft landed, minimising downtime, and increasing efficiency. The system was intended to be the key enabler for any Performance Based Logistics (PBL) arrangements for the F-35.

ALIS was supposed to make maintenance faster, easier, and more predictable, but in service it proved difficult to use and plagued by problems. It was also very expensive. Lockheed's early claims that the F-35 was "designed to achieve unprecedented levels of ▶

'Crew One,' a three-man weapons load team, completes the first full external loadout with live munitions for the F-35A Lightning II May 3, 2019, at Al Dhafra Air Base, United Arab Emirates. F-35A Lightning IIs assigned to the 4th Expeditionary Fighter Squadron were configured with a full external live loadout of six GBU-49 small glide munitions and two AIM-9X Sidewinder missiles to execute an operation in southwest Asia. (Photo: US Air Force)

A US Air Force F-35A Lightning II aircraft assigned to the 48th Fighter Wing at Royal Air Force Lakenheath, during a mission on April 14, 2022. The aircraft is in typical 'Day 2' fit, with external weapons restricted to a pair of AIM-9X Sidewinders on the outboard underwing hardpoints. (Photo: US Air Force, Senior Airman Kevin Long)

An F-35A Lightning II test aircraft assigned to the 31st Test Evaluation Squadron from Edwards Air Force Base, California, fires an AIM-120 AMRAAM at a QF-16 target during a live-fire test over an US Air Force range in the Gulf of Mexico on June 12, 2018. The Joint Operational Test Team conducted the missions as part of Block 3F Initial Operational Test and Evaluation. (Photo: US Air Force)

reliability and maintainability, combined with a highly responsive support and training system linked with the latest in information technology" rang a bit hollow with ALIS, and because logistics support accounts for two-thirds of an aircraft's life cycle cost, this was a serious problem for the F-35.

The F-35 programme is now replacing the much-maligned ALIS logistics system with its sleeker, faster and younger replacement, ODIN, which incorporates a new integrated data environment and a new suite of user-centred applications. While ALIS came in a big electronics box that weighed around 800lb, the new ODIN system comes in two suitcase-

sized cases weighing 100lb, while its increased computing power cut processing times by as much as 50%. ODIN is also a cloud-native system that will allow software engineers to write updates quickly to cope with changing conditions and has been described as turning: "maintenance data into actionable information that enables pilots, maintainers and military leaders to make proactive decisions and keep jets flying."

The OBK (ODIN Base Kit) has been claimed to be 30% cheaper, 75% smaller and 90% lighter than the ALIS SOU (Standard Operating Unit) and has already shown considerable promise. Many believe that ODIN will significantly improve F-35

fleet sustainment, readiness, and availability, while boosting mission capability rates. It also promises to deliver more agile and rapid updates in response to emerging requirements.

Today's F-35A has its roots in a plan for the USAF to field an all-stealth frontline force, with 132 Advanced Technology Bombers (which became the Northrop B-2A Spirit), 750 Advanced Tactical Fighters (these became the Lockheed F-22) and a massive fleet of what were supposed to be much more affordable fighters. There were initially two separate affordable fighter efforts, with the US Air Force and the US Navy initiating the Joint Advanced Strike Technology (JAST) programme in late 1993, and DARPA launching its own Common Affordable Lightweight Fighter (CALF) project. The appearance of the word 'affordable' in one of the acronymic project names was no coincidence, since from the start, the requirements directed a balanced approach to affordability, lethality, survivability, and supportability. These two efforts were subsequently merged, eventually becoming the Joint Strike Fighter programme.

Joint Strike Fighter

The Joint Strike Fighter was designed to replace a number of ageing fighter inventories – initially including US Air Force F-16s and A-10s, US Navy F/A-18s, US Marine Corps AV-8B Harriers and F/A-18s, and UK Harrier GR.Mk 7s and Sea Harriers, though there was felt to be a much bigger potential market for the aircraft among US allies.

After an evaluation of competing designs, there was a fly-off between Boeing's X-32A and Lockheed's X-35, with the System Development

An F-35A shows off a weapons bay packed with four GBU-53B StormBreaker glide bombs and a single AIM-120 AMRAAM. The GBU-53B was previously known as the Small Diameter Bomb II. (Photo: US Air Force)

The development and testing of equipment for F-35A nuclear capability is known as making an aircraft 'dual-capable', meaning that it is able to deliver both conventional and nuclear weapons. Here an F-35A (AF-6) flown by Major Chris 'Beast' Taylor drops an inert B61-12 nuclear weapon during a dual capable aircraft (DCA) test flight in the skies above Edwards Air Force Base, California on 25 November 2019. (Photo: Lockheed Martin, Darin 'Snap' Russell, flight test photographer)

and Demonstration (SDD) contract for what would become the F-35 being awarded to Lockheed Martin on October 26, 2001.

The F-35 was produced in three versions, with the conventional F-35A for the USAF complemented by the F-35B short take off and vertical landing (STOVL) version for the USMC, and the carrier-capable F-35C variant for the navy.

Nine countries participated in the development of the F-35, which represented a new model of international cooperation, while also ensuring the security of the USA and its Coalition partners well into the 21st century. There were three levels of international participation in the F-35 programme, reflecting a member nation's financial stake in the programme, and affecting the amount of technology transfer, the quantity of subcontracts open for bid by national companies, and the order in which countries would be able to obtain production aircraft. The United Kingdom was the sole 'Level 1' partner, contributing US $2.5bn, which was about 10% of the planned development costs under the 1995 Memorandum of Understanding that brought the UK into the project. Italy, and the Netherlands were Level 2 partners contributing $1bn and $800m each, respectively. Level 3 partners were Turkey $195m, Canada US$160m, Australia US$144m, Norway $122m and Denmark $110m.

Edward C. 'Pete' Aldridge Jr, the Under Secretary of Defense for Acquisition, Technology and Logistics, announced the decision to proceed with the Joint Strike Fighter (JSF) programme on October 26, 2001, thereby launching the System Development and Demonstration (SDD) phase. James G. Roche, the Secretary of the Air Force, announced the selection of Lockheed Martin teamed with Northrop Grumman and BAE to develop and then produce the JSF aircraft.

The first F-35A was rolled out at Fort Worth, Texas, on February 19, 2006 and made its maiden flight on December 15 of the same year.

By then, the aircraft had formally been named as the 'Lightning II' with a nod to the Lockheed P-38 Lightning of World War Two. As is so often the case, however, this official name has been widely ignored within the USAF, and the aircraft is informally known as the Panther.

The aircraft's software was progressively released in six releases, or Blocks. The first two Blocks, 1A and 1B, were used for initial pilot training with Block 2A improving the training capability, and Block 2B was used for the USMC's Initial Operating Capability (IOC). Block 3i had the same capabilities as 2B but was hosted on new hardware and was used for early training, and for the USAF's IOC, which was declared by the USAF's 34th Fighter Squadron at Hill Air Force Base, Utah on August 2, 2016.

The F-35A and the USMC F-35B variant were cleared for basic flight training in early 2012, although there were concerns over safety and performance due to lack of system maturity. The USAF began an operational utility evaluation (OUE) of the F-35A, including logistical support, maintenance, and training on September 10, 2012.

USAF pilot training began at Eglin AFB in January 2013 - the USAF F-35A basic training course is held at Eglin AFB and Luke AFB.

By the time IOC was declared, the USAF had suffered its first F-35A loss. On June 23, 2014, an F-35A suffered a serious engine fire at Eglin AFB. The pilot escaped unharmed, but the aircraft sustained an estimated $50m in damage, and the fleet was grounded for nearly two weeks. The USAF Air Education and Training Command (AETC) report was issued In June 2015, and blamed the failure on the third stage rotor of the engine's fan module, pieces of which cut through the fan case and upper fuselage. Pratt & Whitney applied an extended 'rub-in' to increase the gap between the second stator and the third rotor integral arm seal and made design alterations to pre-trench the stator.

F-35As participated in their first Red Flag exercise in 2017, achieving a kill ratio of 15:1 against F-16 aggressors. The first USAF F-35A

overseas deployment, to Al Dhafra Air Base in the UAE, began on April 15, 2019. On April 27, 2019, USAF F-35As involved in this deployment made the type's combat debut, attacking a so-called Islamic State (ISIS) tunnel network in northern Iraq.

The F-35 forms the cornerstone of the USAF's future fighter plans, with a 'programme of record' for 1,763 aircraft, about 302 of which have been delivered. The aircraft is also the mainstay of most allied air forces – and would underpin any future air power coalition. Lockheed Martin claim that the F-35 has never lost a competition in which it has competed for a fighter aircraft order, and certainly the aircraft has achieved real momentum on the export market, such that most of the USA's most important allies now operate the type, providing a useful commonality and interoperability advantage for the USAF, as well as helping to drive down unit costs for the US operator. Lockheed Martin claim that the F-35 thereby "strengthens national security, enhances global partnerships and powers economic growth," while delivering transformational capabilities for 21st century Security. It is hard to argue with these broad conclusions.

The export success of the F-35A may bring its own problems, since this also means that there may be a shortage of non-stealthy allied aircraft that might offer genuinely complimentary capabilities, since even the F-35 can't do everything.

It has also contributed to the relatively slow build-up of the USAF F-35A force, though this has also been thanks in part to continuing programme delays caused by significant challenges in testing, production, performance, and sustainment. The completion of initial operational testing has been delayed several times (not least by problems with the Joint Simulation Environment), preventing a full-rate production decision and not allowing multi-year block buys that could save costs and speed up deliveries.

The F-35 continues to suffer from a number of deficiencies affecting safety, operational ◢

An F-35A Lightning II flown by a 65th Aggressor Squadron (AGRS) pilot takes off for its first flight with a new paint scheme at Nellis Air Force Base, Nevada, on May 26, 2022. The mission of the 65 AGRS is to teach and replicate fifth-generation adversary tactics. (Photo: US Air Force, A1C Josey Blades)

suitability, and effectiveness, as well reliability, availability, and maintainability. These issues continue to directly impact USAF modernisation plans and to delay the retirement schedule for some older tactical aircraft. At current delivery rates, it will take 30 years to deliver the remaining F-35As – leading many to suspect that the eventual number may be lower than was once planned.

The current fleet-standard Block 3F software gives the F-35A full combat capability with a

Two F-16Cs from the 176th Fighter Squadron, from Truax Field ANGB, at Madison with an F-35A wearing the 53rd Wing's 'OT' tail code. Truax Field is one of the next units expected to convert to the Lightning II. (Photo: US Air Force, Scott Wolf)

variety of precision guided weapons allowing the aircraft to perform interdiction, basic CAS, and limited SEAD missions. The new Block 4 modernisation will add new hardware and software and will bring all aircraft to a common fleet configuration, adding 88 new capabilities, correcting deficiencies found in concurrent development/testing, and allowing the integration of new weapons, including the Advanced Anti-Radiation Guided Missile-Extended Range, SDB II, the Stand-in Attack

Weapon (SiAW), and the new B61-12 nuclear weapon. weapon. Integrating these, as well as JASSM, and LRASM, onto the F-35 will continue to expand the aircraft's multi-role mission capabilities – and promises to help to ensure that the F-35 remains the most lethal, stealthy, and survivable aircraft in the world.

The so-called the Technology Refresh 3 (TR-3) package provides updated displays, updated memory, and updated core processing and computer power and will facilitate the full Block 4 upgrade.

The full Block 4 was at one time expected to require a new engine, to provide more electrical power. The F-35A's current Pratt & Whitney F135 engine produces 43,000lb of thrust and consists of a three-stage fan, a six-stage compressor, an annular combustor, a single-stage high-pressure turbine, and a two-stage low-pressure turbine. General Electric Aviation and Pratt & Whitney designed adaptive new engines for the F-35 under the Adaptive Engine Transition Program (AETP), but it was determined that Pratt & Whitney's proposal to modernise the existing F135s under the Engine Core Upgrade was a more cost-efficient option and plans for a new generation adaptive engine have been abandoned.

Units

The 302 F-35As in the inventory in mid-2022 included 282 with active duty units, and 20 with the Air National Guard.

The USAF's F-35A units now include the 33rd Fighter Wing (AETC) and the 53rd Wing (ACC) at Eglin AFB, Florida; the 48th Fighter Wing (USAFE-AFAFRICA) at RAF Lakenheath, UK; the 56th Fighter Wing (AETC) and the 944th Fighter

Wing (AFRC) at Luke AFB, Arizona; the 57th Wing (ACC) and the 926th Wing (AFRC) at Nellis AFB, Nevada; the 354th Fighter Wing (PACAF) at Eielson AFB, Alaska; the 388th Fighter Wing (ACC) and the 419th Fighter Wing (AFRC) at Hill AFB, Utah and the 412th Test Wing (AFMC) at Edwards AFB, California.

The Vermont ANG's 158th Fighter Wing at Burlington ANGB has also re-equipped with the F-35A.

Further Air National Guard F-35A operating locations include Dannelly Field, Alabama and Truax Field, Wisconsin, while one Air Force Reserve location – Naval Air Station Joint Reserve Base Fort Worth, Texas - will also receive F-35As. The next Active Duty F-35A base will be Tyndall AFB, Florida.

Nellis AFB include the 6th Weapons Squadron of the USAF Weapons School, which was activated at Nellis AFB in June 2017 to develop an F-35A weapons instructor curriculum while the 65th Aggressor Squadron was reactivated with the F-35A at the same base in June 2022 to offer expanded training against adversary stealth aircraft.

The F-35 programme is now nearing the end of what has been a long-running, multi-year IOT&E (Initial Operational Test and Evaluation) effort. The JSF Operational Test Team (JOTT) has now completed cold-weather testing; a series of weapons trials (both bombs and missiles); deployments to austere environments; and testing that compared F-35 performance to that of fourth-generation fighters against traditional and more modern surface-to-air threats currently fielded by potential adversaries. Cybersecurity testing of the air vehicle, training systems, mission data reprogramming laboratory, and the Autonomic Logistics Information System (ALIS) has also been completed, but the process has been held up by delays to testing in the DOD's Joint Simulation Environment.

Completion of IOT&E could finally unlock full-rate production thereby allowing cost-saving multiyear block buys. But completion of IOT&E does not indicate that the F-35A's troubles are over.

The official FY2021 report by the Director Operational Test and Evaluation revealed that aircraft availability rates had plateaued during the year and had been declining in the final

An F-35A Lightning II pilot assigned to the 134th Fighter Squadron, Vermont Air National Guard, prepares for launch during routine flying operations at the Vermont Air National Guard base, South Burlington, Vermont, on September 23, 2020. The Vermont Air National Guard began three weeks of night flying operations on April 6, 2021. (Photo: US Air National Guard, A1C Jana Somero)

months of the year, with a sharp reduction in availability since June 2021.

The report also noted that the F-35 fleet remained below Joint Strike Fighter Operational Requirements Document (ORD) thresholds in some areas for overall reliability and maintainability, and that the F-35A was not meeting the full set of ORD reliability and maintainability requirements for mature aircraft.

The F-35's operating cost also remains higher than those of some older USAF tactical aircraft. In fiscal year 2018, the F-35A's cost per flight hour (CPFH) was calculated at $44,000, though the cost reduced to $35,000 in 2019, and Lockheed Martin hopes to reduce it to $25,000 by 2025 through performance-based logistics and other measures. Some doubt that such a reduction is possible, given the maintenance demands of the F-35's LO coatings.

There are hopes that the next Continuous Capability Development and Delivery (C2D2) Block 4 software iteration will correct deficiencies discovered in concurrent development/testing and will add integration of the B61-12 nuclear weapon, SDB II and the

developmental Stand-in Attack Weapon (SiAW), as well as improved sensors, EW, and maritime strike capability. There were suggestions that Block 4 would require a new engine, though plans for this have been put on ice.

With stealth and its complement of next-generation technologies, the mature F-35 promises to be far and away the world's most advanced multi-role fighter. It is perhaps ironic that the US 'tilt to the Pacific' will force the USAF to operate at much longer ranges, and that this may render the tactically-ranged F-35A less relevant than it should have been. Though the F-35's Low Observable characteristics, advanced systems and unparalleled connectivity make it better able to penetrate advanced A2/AD defences and then to strike heavily defended targets, it may lack the range to do so in the Pacific.

And while the F-22 and F-35 were once expected to supplant all fourth-generation fighters, this is no longer going to be the case, and relatively large numbers of ageing F-16s look set to remain in service, while the new build F-15EX will also remain part of the fighter roadmap for years to come. ∎

Lt Col Brent 'Gunner' Reinhardt gets airborne from Edwards AFB, California on April 25, 2013 for a night IMC flight. The F-35 Integrated Test Force made five night flights from Edwards, with another conducted from Patuxent River. (Photo: US Air Force)

This illustration appeared in the official Department of the Air Force Acquisition Biennial Report for 2019 and 2020. Despite this apparent credibility, it probably bears little resemblance to the eventual NGAD manned fighter!
(Photo: US Air Force)

Next Generation Air Dominance

The USAF is betting its future on whatever emerges from the secretive Next Generation Air Dominance (NGAD) programme, though there may only be 200 examples of the manned fighter that will lie at the heart of this system of systems – augmented by larger numbers of unmanned 'collaborative combat aircraft'.

To address short-term and long-term capacity and capability challenges, the USAF is upgrading existing tactical aircraft systems with enhanced capabilities and acquiring new versions of existing platforms. But at the same time, both the air force and US Navy are working on separate Next Generation Air Dominance (NGAD) programmes.

The USAF's Next Generation Air Dominance programme is intended to produce a 'system of systems' that will collectively provide a suite of capabilities – including an advanced manned air dominance fighter aircraft that will replace the F-22 in service. The NGAD family of systems is intended to ensure air superiority in the highly contested future threat environments that were forecast in the 2018 National Defense Strategy.

Work is already underway, with digital engineering and agile software development being used, alongside other new processes and practices, to try to accelerate the process of getting the NGAD capability to the frontline.

As far as is known, no final design (nor contractor) has been down selected, though it has been reported that a demonstrator (and probably not a prototype) has flown in the real world.

NGAD – What we know, and what we think!

The existence of the NGAD programme is openly admitted. Senior officers and government officials even talk about it, in broad terms. But beyond the most broad-brush outline, almost anything else is secret – even

though a demonstrator is said to have been flying since 2020. NGAD is highly classified and is likely to remain so for as long as the air force can manage to keep it hidden. The air force is reluctant to share the shape and features of the NGAD manned combat aircraft to give the USAF's opponents no advanced warning of what they may be facing, and no 'head start' in the development of countermeasures.

NGAD will be one of four key platforms in the USAF's future fighter roadmap, alongside the F-35, F-15EX, and F-16, and is expected to be the key element in ensuring that a smaller fighter force remains relevant and viable, and capable of winning the air superiority fight, even in highly-contested enemy sovereign airspace – the most challenging operational environment.

The F-22 is already flying with the IRST sensor pod shown in this painting, but not yet with the stealthy fuel tanks shown, nor the AIM-260 JATM. This configuration will 'bridge the gap' pending the service entry of NGAD. (Photo: US Air Force)

Major General Scott Jobe, director of the US Air Force Air Combat Command plans, programs and requirements directorate has said that: "We're going to field a capability that has lethal characteristics and can both penetrate and persist long-range. That is what brings air superiority."

By 2030, the air force believes that its F-22 Raptors may no longer be sufficiently survivable in contested air space, while there is already concern that it may lack the range and persistence to be relevant in any conflict with China in the Pacific.

In short, NGAD will be a penetrating counter air system with multi-domain awareness, agile resilient communications, and an integrated family of capabilities.

Although the F-22 is still considered to be the best air dominance fighter in the world, there are no plans to retain it once NGAD has been deployed in significant numbers. This means that any upgrades to the F-22 will be limited to those necessary to keep the Raptor viable as an interim air dominance solution.

Some, including Heritage Foundation think tank fellow and former air force fighter pilot John Venable, believe that early withdrawal of F-22a may be unwise. "If it does not happen, and this slides into the next decade — which is more likely than not — it would be a fool's errand to actually cash in viable combat platforms now on a bet that no Las Vegas gambler would take," he told *Defense News*. ▶

NGAD is a system of systems, and though there will be a new manned fighter at the heart of it, the various adjuncts and effectors will also be used with the F-35A. (Photo: Lockheed Martin)

A number of testbeds are already flying various NGAD technologies. This F-22 is believed to be testing new LO coatings developed for the NGAD programme. (Photo: Steve Fortson)

The need for a system of systems had been highlighted in a 2014 DARPA Air Dominance Initiative study, which concluded that "no single new technology or platform could deter and defeat the sophisticated and numerous adversary systems under development." The Air Superiority 2030 flight plan produced by the air force enterprise capability collaboration team reached the same conclusion, noting that: "There is no single capability that provides a silver bullet solution."

In September 2019, Gen David Goldfein, the then-chief of staff of the US Air Force, endorsed the same approach, saying: "Here's our NGAD strategy: We have five key technologies that we're investing in that we don't intend to have all come together on a single platform," Goldfein said. "They will all mature and accelerate at difference paces. As they become ready, you will see us adapting them on existing platforms, sensors and weapons and also looking at new platforms, sensors, and weapons."

System of systems

Major General Jobe confirmed last year that, in order to meet the 'peer level threat', NGAD will be a 'family of systems'.

"NGAD is not a single capability that is easily targeted; it is not a single platform, a single weapon or a single planning issue," Jobe said. "It is intended to be a deliberate solution to complicate targeting for an enemy."

In saying this, Jobe was echoing Frank Kendall, the Secretary of the Air Force, who has said that: "NGAD must be more than just the next crewed fighter jet. It's a programme that will include a crewed platform teamed with much less expensive autonomous uncrewed combat aircraft, employing a distributed, tailorable mix of sensors, weapons, and other mission equipment operating as a team or formation."

This mix of platforms and systems (some of them manned, others unmanned, and some of them operating from space) will collaboratively gain air dominance in combat.

This system of systems approach is a critical component of the USAF's future long-range kill chain, and echoes what France, Germany, and Spain are doing with their SCAF future air dominance programme, and what the UK, Japan, Italy, and Sweden are pursuing with the GCAP project.

Exquisite technologies

The USAF is focused on fielding capabilities to mitigate identified gaps in its overall ability to win air dominance and not necessarily on creating a 'next generation' aircraft, and the central manned NGAD platform may be relatively conservative – perhaps even based on the airframe of the B-21, if we are to believe Former Air Combat Command commander Gen Herbert 'Hawk' Carlisle, who speculated in 2017 that the 'Penetrating Combat Aircraft' (NGAD's precursor) could be something like the B-21 bomber, whose big wings and big fuel tanks suited it well for the long ranges of the Pacific theatre while its capacious bomb bays promised a greater magazine capacity for the internal carriage of more AAMs. Most of the concept art seen so far does show a tailless

This Boeing 737 is one of a number of large aircraft testbeds for NGAD systems, sensors, and avionics. It has not been painted since rolling off the Boeing production line! (Photo: Alan Hess)

This F-35C is believed to be another LO coatings testbed, almost certainly gathering data in support of the NGAD programme. (Photo: Fred Taleghani)

platform, but one with a more sharply swept delta platform, looking more 'fighter like'.

But whatever shape the NGAD platform, it will incorporate multiple new technologies. It will leverage the five key technologies referred to by the then Air Force Chief of Staff General Goldfein in 2019 (hypersonics, directed energy, long-range fires, precision fires, space capabilities), and many others, and the whole NGAD family is expected to be 'orders of magnitude' stealthier than today's fifth-generation LO aircraft.

As well as an adaptive-cycle propulsion system, the NGAD family of systems is likely to require more advanced communications and networking systems, more onboard electrical-power generation, and better thermal management to reduce signature, as well as advanced LO technologies. The aircraft will use new generation sensors including advanced passive detection systems, and new types of armament perhaps including directed-energy weapons.

These may be more of a feature of future iterations of NGAD, since today's laser systems (e.g., those being developed under the Self-protect High-Energy Laser Demonstrator (SHiELD) programme) are only capable of generating about 150kw of focused power. This is barely sufficient to protect aircraft against incoming missiles, by blinding or over-heating their seekers.

The first generation of NGAD is likely to be more conventionally armed. The main BVR air-to-air weapon is likely to be the AIM-260A Joint Advanced Tactical Missile (JATM), now under development by Lockheed Martin. The JATM was meant to counter China's long-range PL-15 air-to-air missile and give the US the kind of 'first shot, first kill' advantage it once enjoyed with AMRAAM. The missile has similar dimensions to the AIM-120, and employs a dual pulse rocket motor, and not a throttleable ramjet like the class-leading Meteor.

JATM may be only an interim weapon for NGAD, since the Long-Range Engagement Weapon (LREW), being developed by Raytheon, and the Long Range Air-to-Air Missile (LRAAM), being developed by Boeing may be used, if they reach service.

The more compact Raytheon Peregrine and Lockheed Martin Cuda could also play a part, perhaps allowing NGAD adjuncts to carry a meaningful BVR air-to-air weapon.

Northrop Grumman is actively promoting its new software-controlled, multimode, 'ultra-wideband' EMRIS (Electronically scanned Multifunction Reconfigurable Integrated Sensor) for a number of applications, possibly including the US Air Force Collaborative Combat Aircraft and/or the Next-Generation Air Dominance (NGAD) manned fighter. Northrop claim that the new

sensor can simultaneously conduct radar, communications, and electronic warfare tasks.

The precise make-up of the NGAD system of systems is still undefined. It is known that the Collaborative Combat Aircraft (CCA) programme is intended to field one or more unmanned aircraft types as a component of the Next Generation Air Dominance family of systems, but the precise number and nature of adjuncts and effectors has not been made public.

Frank Kendall's vision envisages as many as five unmanned systems flying with the manned combat aircraft performing strike, Intelligence, Surveillance and Reconnaissance (ISR), and electronic warfare missions or serving as decoys to draw fire, or as expendable effectors in their own right.

These would be employed as an integrated part of a unit - perhaps at squadron level.

USAF Pacific Commander General Kenneth Wilsbach has suggested that the adjuncts could be used for penetrating strike missions in an A2AD (Anti Access/Area Denial) environment.

Kendall has said that the USAF wants those unmanned aircraft to cost no more than half as much as their manned counterparts, leading some to assume that he meant half as much as the NGAD's manned component (which are expected to cost several hundred million dollars each), meaning that NGAD loyal wingmen might cost as much or more than an F-35. In fact, ▶

Two similar configurations were apparent in this official rendering from 2020, one with a cranked leading edge, one a pure Delta. (Photo: US Air Force)

inside 12 to 15 years, rather than the usual 30 to 40 year lifespan. New, more advanced types will be developed roughly every five to eight years. Hinote would not "confirm or deny" that the second NGAD model is already in development.

NGAD will not replace the F-22 on a one-for-one basis, with the USAF acquiring 100 or fewer of the first NGAD version before moving on to its successor. This rapid, more iterative, and frequent development cycle would replace the "winner-take-all" competitions typified by the F-22 and F-35 programmes. This fast-turn sequential development will allow what Hinote called "the great companies of our industrial base to re-enter the competition at the design phase", rather than being locked out of what can be a 50 year development/production/sustainment programme until the next generational shift and the next major procurement competition.

High Cost

When asked about the unit price of the manned element of NGAD during an appearance before the House Armed Services Committee, Air Force Secretary Frank Kendall did not answer directly, saying only that each piloted aircraft was expected to cost "multiple" hundreds of millions of dollars, and that NGAD could be the most expensive aircraft programme in history. Later asked whether the US could afford an air platform costing multiple hundreds of millions

the air force wants these aircraft to cost no more than half as much as an F-35, making the most expensive CCA variants around $40m, while Kendall has said that he would like to spend "a factor less than that."

This might mitigate against the use of larger, more capable 'Loyal Wingmen' in the mould of the Boeing MQ-28 Ghost Bat (or the UK's abandoned Mosquito) in favour of smaller adjuncts, and it is perhaps significant that Lockheed Martin have outlined a multi-layered 'distributed team' of diverse unmanned aircraft working in concert with manned types, and which did not include a traditional 'loyal wingman' concept.

Whatever emerges from the CCA project will not be exclusively used alongside NGAD and will be used to complement other systems and platforms (especially the F-35), though they are being developed specifically to augment NGAD. Some will be escorts carrying sensors or more weapons, while others will provide electronic or ground attack capabilities in order to enable NGAD to penetrate enemy defences and hold any target in the battlespace at risk. Some elements of the system may even be optionally

manned. All platforms could be directed by the pilot of an F-35, or "from a seat on the E-7 Wedgetail," or from a KC-46 tanker, or ground station.

The competition for the Collaborative Combat Aircraft (CCA) programme is expected to be launched in Fiscal Year 2024.

Development of NGAD will follow an ambitious timeline – and it may never be built in large numbers. We can expect rapid development and deployment, as the USAF has placed a premium on agility to meet a rapidly changing and evolving threat.

The NGAD programme is described as using a "non-traditional acquisition approach to avoid traditional monolithic program schedules and exorbitant life-cycle sustainment costs." This Digital Century Series approach, "creates a realistic business case for industry to adopt commercial best practises for key design activities – before a part is even manufactured."

Under the Digital Century Series model, multiple types of aircraft will be developed and fielded successively in small production runs (of perhaps 50 to 100 aircraft), with each type being introduced, operated, and retired

of dollars — several times the price tag of an F-35 fighter — Kendall answered by asking: "Can the nation afford not to have air superiority? We have to have air superiority."

In December 2018, the Congressional Budget Office (CBO) forecast that the first of 414 PCA aircraft would enter service in 2030, at an average cost of about $300m each, with an overall procurement cost of $130bn between 2028 and 2050. Since then, though, the NGAD concept has been reframed, and under the Digital Century Series approach, aircraft numbers have been reduced, but so too has the budget – reducing from $13.2bn during the five-year period from fiscal 2020-24 to $6.1bn for the same period. But unit cost will still be high, by any standards.

While the upfront 'sticker price' of NGAD will be high, it seems that real efforts are being made to hold sustainment costs down in the long term, Kendall has said. This is being achieved by using modular designs and government-controlled interfaces to ensure ease of maintenance and upgrade, and to allow competitive sustainment. Also, the short, planned service life of the NGAD manned aircraft will further reduce through life support costs. Today, manufacturers make most of their money from sustainment, rather than from design, development, and production, those behind the new NGAD approach aim to turn that on its head, and to eliminate 'vendor lock', ensuring that the original manufacturer no longer exercises monopolistic control of sustainment.

When Lockheed promoted its US-built A330 MRTT derivative, the LMXT, it showed an NGAD fighter being refuelled. This bears some resemblance to the manned NGF fighter at the centre of the Franco-Germano-Spanish SCAF programme. (Photo: Lockheed Martin)

Dr Will Roper, the Assistant Secretary of the Air Force for Acquisition, Technology and Logistics, officially stood up the Program Executive Office for Advanced Aircraft during a ceremony at Wright-Patterson Air Force Base, on October 2, 2019. This office will be tasked with transforming the Next Generation Air Dominance programme into the air force's Digital Century Series initiative, using digital engineering, modular open systems architecture, and agile software development to design advanced aircraft faster and bring them into production with a significantly lower learning curve.

NGAD funding has been in place since 2015, and numerous air force officers and officials have talked about fielding NGAD by as early as 2030. This would seem at best ambitious, and ➤

Lockheed's NGAD concept seems to emphasise speed and stealth, with a sharply swept leading edge and low observable engine nozzles. (Photo: Lockheed Martin)

Among the adjuncts studied for NGAD are a number of unmanned weapons carriers such as this DARPA concept. An aircraft like this could save the manned fighter from having to go too far into contested airspace. (Photo: DARPA)

at worst completely unrealistic, given that on March 3, 2022, Secretary of the Air Force Frank Kendall told the Air Force Association's Warfare Symposium that defining the Next Generation Air Dominance (NGAD) System-of-Systems was one of his department's 'seven operational imperatives', implying that the project was still at the definition stage, rather than the development stage.

In June 2022, Kendall publicly said that the NGAD programme had already started its EMD (engineering, manufacturing, and development) phase, but rowed back from that in September, confirming that the NGAD platform was still in design and had not formally entered engineering, manufacturing, and development, and had not gone through its preliminary design review and that the Milestone B decision (which is a prerequisite for entering the EMD phase) had not been taken.

The Milestone B review marks the completion of a programme's technology maturation phase and the formal start of an acquisition programme. The USAF would then take the preliminary design and focus on system integration, manufacturing processes and other details ahead of production. The Milestone C decision then comes at the end of the EMD phase when the decision is made as to whether to move to production and deployment.

Kendall has said that the average air force acquisition programme takes a little less than seven years to move from starting EMD to achieving initial operating capability, though the F-35 took 15 years. Kendall told the Air, Space and Cyber conference, that the NGAD timeline might be further compressed, noting that: "I'm not sure NGAD will be an average programme."

Kendall has said that he is pushing acquisition officials to get new capabilities, such as the Collaborative Combat Aircraft, into the field faster than is normally possible. "I have a sense of urgency about getting new capabilities [and] I'm willing to take some risk there," he averred.

The three US major defence aerospace primes, Boeing, Lockheed Martin, and Northrop Grumman are believed to still be competing to build the manned sixth-generation fighter that will serve as the centrepiece of the NGAD system of systems.

In August 2022, the USAF awarded five companies - General Electric (GE) Aviation, Pratt & Whitney (P&W), Boeing, Lockheed Martin, and Northrop Grumman - an indefinite-delivery,

This Boeing concept artwork shows two MQ-28 loyal wingmen with an F-15EX. The various elements of the NGAD system of systems will work alongside the NGAD manned fighter and legacy assets. (Photo: Boeing)

indefinite-quantity contract for the prototyping phase of the Next Generation Adaptive Propulsion (NGAP) programme.

Flying already?

Though no photos of the aircraft have emerged, it is known that a full-scale demonstrator aircraft has flown. In 2019, General Goldfein told *Aviation Week*'s Steve Trimble that: "There has to be a test article to be able to take some of these technologies to maturity, but that's probably about as far as I can go."

In 2020 the USAF's then top acquisition official, Will Roper, said that: "NGAD right now is designing, assembling, testing, and, in the digital world, exploring things that would have cost us time and money to wait for physical world results... The announcement isn't that we just built an e-plane and have flown it a lot of times in a virtual world, which we've done. But if you think that we don't care about physical-world results, we do. In fact, NGAD has come so far that the full-scale flight demonstrator has already flown in the physical world. We've already built and flown a full-scale flight demonstrator in the real world, and we broke records in doing it. We are ready to go and build the next-generation aircraft in a way that has never happened before."

Frank Kendall has said that: "What we did was an experimental prototype. We basically had an X plane programme which was designed to reduce the risk of some of the key technologies that we would need for a production programme."

Lockheed is investing $100m in distributed teaming technologies under Project Carrera. Survivable crewed platforms, like the F-35, will be partnered with affordable, modular uncrewed assets, like the company's Speed Racer drone. (Photo: Lockheed Martin)

This may have been a reference to DARPA's little-known Aerospace Innovation Initiative (AII), launched in fiscal 2015, but which then disappeared from view – perhaps after moving to the black world. When launched, the Aerospace Innovation Initiative was intended: "to develop and fly two X-plane prototypes that demonstrate advanced technologies for future aircraft. Teams will compete to produce the X-plane prototypes, one focused on future navy operational capabilities and the other on future air force operational capabilities."

General Hinote admits to having taken "cleared members of Congress to see the aircraft," who, he said, came away "impressed." According to Hinote, the test pilots flying the NGAD demonstrator also gave it high marks. ■

Lockheed
F-117A Nighthawk

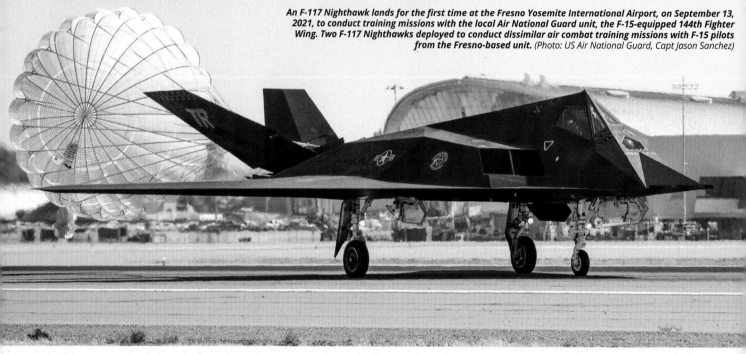

An F-117 Nighthawk lands for the first time at the Fresno Yosemite International Airport, on September 13, 2021, to conduct training missions with the local Air National Guard unit, the F-15-equipped 144th Fighter Wing. Two F-117 Nighthawks deployed to conduct dissimilar air combat training missions with F-15 pilots from the Fresno-based unit. (Photo: US Air National Guard, Capt Jason Sanchez)

The F-117A Nighthawk was born in the 'black world', operating in complete secrecy for the first years of its life. It has been doing much the same since its supposed 'retirement' in 2008, and in September 2022 the Air Force Test Center published a Request For Information (RFI) concerning a 10-year contract for maintenance and logistics support services for the F-117A fleet implying that the US Air Force is planning to keep the aircraft flying until at least 2034.

Officially retired from USAF service on April 22, 2008, but still in use to this day, the Lockheed F-117A Nighthawk was the world's first operational stealth aircraft. Developed in secret, the aircraft was initially deployed under 'Black World' conditions, unadmitted and unacknowledged, operating by night with an elaborate cover story disguising what the operating unit, then known as the 4450th Tactical Group, actually did for a living.

And the F-117A's role was one of striking critical, heavily defended targets with precision guided weapons, using its LO (Low Observable) characteristics to penetrate dense threat environments. Primary missions included precision attack, air interdiction, SEAD, and special operations.

The highly classified F-117A development and manufacturing effort began in November 1978, and the first of five YF-117A 'Senior Trend' prototypes made its maiden flight on June 18, 1981. To lower development costs, the avionics, fly-by-wire systems, and other

systems and parts were derived from the General Dynamics F-16 Fighting Falcon, Boeing B-52 Stratofortress, McDonnell Douglas F/A-18 Hornet, and McDonnell Douglas F-15E Strike Eagle. The parts for the F-117A programme were originally described as spares for these aircraft in budgetary requests, helping to keep the F-117 project secret.

Such was the secrecy and compartmentalisation within the Black World that the weapon developed for the aircraft, the GBU-24 Paveway III (itself originally developed in secret) did not fit the F-117A's bomb bay! This required the rapid development of the GBU-27, which used the smaller tail unit of the Paveway II.

The first production F-117A was delivered in 1982, and operational capability was achieved in October 1983. The type remained secret, ensuring that had it been used 'plausible deniability' might have been achieved. Pilots called it simply 'the Black Jet', or 'the Asset'. Policies changed, and the aircraft's existence

was officially revealed on November 10, 1988, when Assistant Secretary of Defense J. Daniel Howard displayed a grainy photograph during a Pentagon press conference. This allowed pilots to begin flying the F-117A in daylight and allowed the 4450th to discard the A-7s that had been its cover story, using the T-38 for training and as a 'hack'.

The unveiling of the F-117A allowed the aircraft to be relocated from its original home in the isolated Tonopah Test Range in Nevada, moving to Holloman AFB in 1992 and coming under the command of the 49th Fighter Wing.

Combat Debut

As far as can be ascertained, the F-117A made its combat debut during Operation Just Cause, the US invasion of Panama in 1989. Two F-117A Nighthawks dropped two bombs on Rio Hato airfield. The aircraft subsequently played a major role in Operation Desert Storm, flying 1,300 sorties and scoring direct hits on 1,600 high-value targets in Iraq. It was inaccurately

An F-117 Nighthawk drops a GBU-28 guided bomb unit during the 'live-fire' weapons testing Combat Hammer exercise, at Hill Air Force Base, Utah. Many believe that the F-117A's retention may have hinged on its status as a LO platform that could drop laser-guided bombs. (Photo: US Air Force)

claimed that "the F-117 was the only airplane that the planners dared risk over downtown Baghdad."

A single F-117A was lost to enemy action during Operation Allied Force, being shot down on March 27, 1999, by a Yugoslav version of the Soviet Isayev S-125 'Neva' (NATO SA-3 'Goa') anti-aircraft missile system. The F-117A went on to serve in Operation Enduring Freedom in 2001 and Operation Iraqi Freedom in 2003 but was prematurely retired in FY 2008 to release funding for the F-22 programme.

The first six aircraft to be retired made their last flights on March 12, 2007, after a ceremony at Holloman AFB to commemorate the aircraft's career. The withdrawal occurred in eight phases, with the operational aircraft retired to Tonopah in seven waves from March 13, 2007, until the last wave's arrival on April 22, 2008. Most of the F-117s were then placed in 'Type 1000' storage in their original climate-controlled hangars at the Tonopah Test Range Airport, with their wings removed to allow multiple aircraft to be stored in what had been single-aircraft shelters, maintained "in a condition that would allow recall of that aircraft to future service."

Four aircraft were briefly retained by the 410th Flight Test Squadron at Palmdale for flight test duties, the last of them being retired to Tonopah on August 11, 2008. And that should have been that. On September 11, 2017, it was reported that the Air Force would remove four F-117s every year to fully divest the fleet, but this does not seem to have happened.

Instead, F-117s were spotted flying periodically from 2014, perhaps merely to keep them in the condition required by the congressional mandate that demanded the possibility of a "recall of that aircraft to future service."

In March 2019, there were unconfirmed reports that four F-117As had been secretly deployed to the Middle East in 2016 where one had been forced to make an emergency landing at Ali Al Salem (OKAS), Kuwait. ▶

Two F-15C Eagles and an F-117 fly in formation over the skies of Fresno, California before breaking to land at the Fresno Yosemite International Airport on September 14, 2021. F-117As were being seen regularly before this more 'official' reveal of the type, which had notionally retired in 2008. (Photo: US Air National Guard, Capt Jason Sanchez)

An F-117 Nighthawk lands at the Fresno Yosemite International Airport on September 15, 2021, after conducting a training mission with F-15Cs from the local Air National Guard unit. The F-117A is understood to have an aggressor role nowadays, standing in for aircraft such as the Chinese J-20 fighter. (Photo: US Air National Guard, Capt Jason Sanchez)

F-117As were photographed several times in 2019, one being spotted wearing an 'aggressor type' colour scheme, another with new unit markings, including a tail band bearing the name 'Dark Knights'. The USAF resolutely refused to comment about the aircraft until September 2021, though there were reports that roughly six of the stored F-117As were airworthy at any given time being flown by contractor and possibly air force pilots.

On September 13, 2021, a pair of F-117s landed at Fresno Yosemite International Airport in California, triggering some official acknowledgement of the type's continued existence, including the release of the accompanying images. The F-117As were deployed to train with the F-15C/D Eagles of the California Air National Guard's 144th Fighter Wing and a press release was issued, confirming that the 144th FW's F-15 pilots would conduct multiple dissimilar air combat training missions with the F-117 pilots. It was subsequently stated that the USAF was using the F-117A aircraft for training and for research,

and that Air Force Test Center personnel were flying them. Interestingly, the aircraft (like several of those photographed in recent years) wore a 'Dark Knights' unit badge on their starboard engine intakes, with their original markings to port.

In a further public acknowledgement of the F-117A's continuing existence, *Air Force Magazine* - a quasi-official publication of the Air and Space Forces Association - listed the F-117A in its 2022 Air and Space Forces Almanac, published in June 2022. ∎

F-117 Nighthawks on the flightline of the 144th Fighter Wing located at Fresno Air National Guard Base, California on September 15, 2021. As well as acting as 'stealthy' aggressors, the F-117As have been used for test and trials work. (Photo: US Air National Guard, Capt Jason Sanchez)